Thy Kingdom Come

Thy Kingdom Come

Walking in Our Godly Inheritance

Dee Alei

Sovereign World

Sovereign World Ltd
PO Box 777
Tonbridge
Kent TN11 0ZS
England

ISBN 1 85240 363 2

Cover design by CCD, www.ccdgroup.co.uk
Typeset by CRB Associates, Reepham, Norfolk
Printed in the United States of America

Contents

Dedication

This book is dedicated to Justin and Lauren. I could not be more proud of you both! You have become living epistles who exemplify His heart – a real man and woman of God. Don't stop there, however. Allow Him to take you deeper, higher, wider . . . because there is always more!

To our many "adopted kids" scattered throughout the United States and England, this book is also dedicated to you. I pray you will never be satisfied with mediocrity! Dez, let the Lord have it *all* and see what mighty and incredible things He will do in and through you. You have only seen the beginning. Jill, may you continue to press in, your eyes ever upon Him, to lay hold of all that Jesus died to purchase for you (Philippians 3:8–14). Erleen, remember that it is never too late when you are dealing with God. Rebecca, just go for it!

Finally, *Thy Kingdom Come* is dedicated to the bride of Christ being prepared by God to reign with Him eternally. It is for those who feel empty, weak and powerless, but who hunger and thirst for more – more of God and more of His life and power in their lives. It is a book dedicated to those who desire to more fully apprehend the inheritance God has purposed for us as co-heirs with Christ.

About the Author

Dee Alei has worked in a team ministry alongside her husband, Dave, for the past 14 years. She is an ordained minister, a pastor, counselor and teacher of the Word who longs to see individuals equipped and released to fulfill the plan and destiny God has for their lives. With a special place in her heart for the hungry and broken, Dee endeavors to bring encouragement and vision to those who feel stagnant, overlooked or disqualified. She has most recently returned to the States after 6 years in the northeast of England where she and her husband Dave were involved in church planting, youth work and equipping the Body of Christ. In *Thy Kingdom Come*, Dee writes with a prophetic anointing and a pastor's heart, challenging us move on in God to embrace the fullness of the inheritance He has for us as His children. Her fervent prayer is that the Body of Christ might **arise** and step into that place of intimacy and authority that the Lord purposed for His Church from before the foundation of the world. She and Dave currently reside near Albuquerque, New Mexico.

Chapter 1

A Divine Wake-up Call

The Lord recently gave me a mental picture of the Church. We were like children wearing cardboard armor, running about waving our cardboard swords and taking ourselves very seriously indeed! I could see the Lord's paternal smile as He looked upon our efforts. The gentleness of His Father's heart was evident, yet it was tinged with a subtle sadness that appeared almost wistful. As I studied His expression, I came to understand that there is an ache in His heart for His children because, in many respects, we are living in a fantasy world. We have convinced ourselves that we know and are walking in the truth. We are quite sure we are strong and mighty, when the reality is often somewhat different. We like to believe that we are possessing and demonstrating things of His kingdom that we still do not understand. Finally, I sensed that His heart is grieved for us because we are generally satisfied with the pretense!

There is a yearning in the heart of God to see His children grow up and transition from the fantasy of childhood play to the reality of what He died to purchase for us. There is an awesome inheritance called the kingdom of God ready and waiting for those who will put away childish things. It is an inheritance available to His children *now* and constitutes the abundant life He came to bring us. Scripture describes the kingdom of God as *"righteousness, peace and joy in the Holy Spirit"* (Romans 14:17). It is a spiritual dimension we can enter and walk in more fully as we increasingly surrender our hearts and lives to the King of kings. Jesus instructed His disciples to pray, *"Your kingdom come"*

(Matthew 6:10), and admonished them to *"seek first the kingdom of God"* (Matthew 6:33). He knew that His kingdom would only become a reality in their lives if they sought it, prayed for it, and were willing to fight for it. The same is true for His disciples today. However, we need a divine dissatisfaction with the status quo to shake some things loose in our lives! His kingdom inheritance will only become ours if we are willing to relinquish all pretense and any illusions we have blithely embraced.

Truth or illusion

The film, *The Matrix*, was a story about artificial intelligence taking over the world, resulting in human beings being grown as a source of energy for machines. These captive humans lived in a virtual reality world that was part of a computer program called "the matrix". In the film, there were three types of people. There were those who were blind and ignorant of reality, but never knew it. All they had ever known was the illusion of life in the matrix. Secondly, there were those who came to know the truth about reality and subsequently embraced it, willing to sacrifice their own comfort for the truth. Finally, there were those who experienced the reality but chose the fantasy world instead because the reality was too stark, too harsh, and too hard.

In many ways, the Body of Christ is like this third group of people in the movie. All too often, we choose to live in a pretend world of illusion because, let's face it, it is so much easier! Illusion is empty, insubstantial and requires nothing of us. We can conform the illusion to whatever we *want* to believe. Truth, however, is well defined and unbending. By its very nature, truth demands something of us and requires an adjustment on our part if we choose to embrace it. Jesus said He is *the* Truth (John 14:6). He called His Spirit "the Spirit of truth" three times in John's gospel. Serving the One who is the embodiment of truth necessarily requires a yielding of our wills to His. He doesn't adjust to us. We must adjust to Him!

However, it is human nature to allow self to dictate our beliefs and our choices, for it is the path of least resistance. Perhaps this is why Jesus said many of us choose the broad path leading to destruction but few choose the narrow way leading to life (Matthew 7:13–14). Consequently, we often choose the illusion, embracing a spirit of deception rather than the Spirit of truth. Such delusion characterized the church at Laodicea (Revelation 3). The risen Lord advised them,

> *"Because you say, 'I am rich, have become wealthy, and have need of nothing' – and do not know that you are wretched, miserable, poor, blind and naked – I counsel you to buy from Me gold refined in the fire, that you may be rich; and white garments, that you may be clothed, that the shame of your nakedness might not be revealed; and anoint your eyes with eye salve, that you may see. As many as I love, I rebuke and chasten. Therefore, be zealous and repent."*   (Revelation 3:17–19)

The church of Laodicea was a lot like the modern western Church in terms of their lukewarm spiritual condition and their capacity for self-deception. We often see ourselves as full of the Spirit of God, enriched with His gifts and emblazoned with His anointing. We think we know exactly what He wants and what this Christian walk is all about. Yet, in so many ways we too are wretched, miserable, poor, blind and naked! Is it any wonder that the Father looks upon us with a trace of sadness in His gaze? Jesus wept over Jerusalem. Perhaps He is weeping over us as well. We think we are in a different place than the religious world of Jesus' day, but is that really the case? Is it truth or illusion? This is a hard question, but a question which I believe is critical to pose in this hour.

Seeing our need

Several years ago, I studied at length the concept of humility. The Lord had been talking to me about humility and I wanted to understand what He meant by it. The best definition I came up with in my study was "seeing our need for God in every area of our lives." Humility is seeing our own fallibility, our bankruptcy, our emptiness, our inability *but for God*. It is recognizing our complete and total need for Him in every area of our lives! This need *for* Him translates into a dependence *upon* Him. So many of us were taught whilst growing up that God helps those who help themselves and that we must pull ourselves up by our bootstraps. This could not be further from God's thinking and ways! This worldly philosophy really teaches independence from God. Pride at its root is simply independence which says, "I can do it; I don't need Your help in this area, Lord."

It is such a part of our carnal nature to operate in independence. I remember when Lauren, our daughter, was two years old. She would shake off my attempts to guide her, saying, "Do it myself!" or "Mommy, I do it!" She was so cute with her big brown eyes and pouting little lips, but so stubborn and independent! Even as grownups, are we really any different?

Lately, the Lord has been teaching us more about the need for utter and total dependence on Him – for everything. Here is an example. When the Lord sent us to the northeast of England, we lived and ministered in a completely different culture than the one in which we were raised. Even the language, a hybrid dialect of English, Scots and Scandinavian languages called Geordie, was different! For the first two or three years, people were very gracious with us because we were so new to the country and in obvious need of some help. Subsequently, however, with deepening relationships and the work that the Lord was doing in our midst, there came the need for greater fine-tuning in our communication with people. We found the cultural and language barrier to be a real stumbling block at times in reaching that place of spiritual unity to which the Lord was calling us. He allowed us to encounter this obstacle as part of our kingdom training. Through the difficulties we faced, He worked in us a dependence upon Him for even the "little" things that we would normally take for granted, such as our communication with other people!

A more recent example involved my attempt to eat more moderately and shed unwanted pounds. I decided one day that I was going to change my eating habits in order to regain the slimmer figure I had once had. I was weary of hurting joints, lethargy and clothes that were too tight! I also tired very easily and found it difficult to keep up with the pace of our ministry schedule. So I developed a common sense plan of action that was sure to drop pounds slowly over a period of time. After a month or so of very carefully monitoring everything I ate and changing my eating habits fairly significantly, there had been no accompanying weight loss. In my discouragement, I went to the Lord and began to pour out my feelings of hopeless and despair to

Him. He gently pointed out that I was trying to do this in my own strength. I had never sought Him about it or invited Him to be a part of it in any way. I had independently set my course of action and was trying to accomplish the goal all by myself. I instantly asked His forgiveness as well as His help, submitting the whole thing to Him. Much to my chagrin, a significant change in weight was observable within the next week! He impressed upon me, once again through this experience, my need for complete and utter dependence upon Him.

The Laodicean church was independent and proud. Pride is characteristic of so much of the modern Church world as well. *"God resists the proud. But gives grace to the humble"* (James 4:6; 1 Peter 5:5). If we have noticed a lack of God's grace in areas of our lives, perhaps we should examine ourselves with a willingness to see if pride is there. Could we be seeing little change because God Himself is resisting us? I've been staggered recently at the amount of pride I still see in myself. Just when I think it has been eradicated from my life, there it appears again! I loathe it when I see it, but I know the Lord hates it even more than I do because it is an open door for bondage.

In contrast to our general perception that we are liberated and free, I believe the Church is still held captive by a great deal of pride, self-deception, idolatry and a host of other things! Just as the giant Gulliver was incapacitated by the ropes woven over him by the tiny men of Lilliput while he was asleep, the Church has been neutralized while we slumbered in our apathy and carelessness. Though this may sound like a negative pronouncement to some, I believe the Lord in His love and mercy is giving us a wake-up call. As the Apostle Paul wrote to the Roman church,

> *" . . . knowing the time, that now it is high time to awake out of sleep; for now our salvation is nearer than when we first believed. The night is far spent, the day is at hand. Therefore let us cast off the works of darkness, and let us put on the armor of light."*
> (Romans 13:11–12)

We have had plenty of ear tickling. I believe He is saying it is time to get real and get honest. He has so much more for us than we have ever imagined, but we will never pursue anything further as long as we are convinced we have already found it!

▶ *Our godly inheritance will only become a reality in our lives as we see our desperate need for more of God in every area of our lives.*

Arising to victory

God's Word is full of promises that He made not only to His people in ancient times, but are also promises for us today if we have opened our hearts and lives to invite Him in. If we have come into covenant with God by the blood of His Son, there is a New Covenant inheritance ready and waiting for us! He has *qualified* us by the provision made at Calvary to become partakers of this inheritance (Colossians 1:12). Under His will, He has bequeathed to us freedom, physical and emotional healing, deliverance, strength, purity, His love, enduring mercy, all sufficient grace, boldness, the fruit of the Spirit, a sound mind, wisdom, supernatural enabling, abundant life, and so much more! In fact, He said that what He has for us is beyond what we have ever seen or heard (1 Corinthians 2:9), and above all that we could ask or even imagine (Ephesians 3:20). That is mind-boggling! Yet our Father, in His perfect wisdom, has not allowed us to be born with the proverbial silver spoon in our mouths. As all good fathers teach their children responsibility, our heavenly Father has said throughout His Word, "Dear children, I will if you will." So much of what He has for us is conditional on our attitudes and response to Him. It is so simple! Responding in obedience to Him leads to freedom and blessing. Passivity in our response to Him leads, very subtly, to spiritual captivity.

Isaiah prophesied of the Babylonian captivity of Judah many years before it happened. In the time he lived, Judah was experiencing increased prosperity and power, and outwardly things looked good. Inwardly, however, there was a serious spiritual decline happening. Isaiah saw judgement coming. He saw the captivity that God would allow, but he also saw the deliverance and redemption that the Lord would ultimately bring through it all. As a young Christian, I had a spiritual mentor who helped me to see that God's judgements upon His people *"are unto victory"* (Matthew 12:20, KJV). It changed my whole way of looking at the Lord's discipline and corrective hand in my life. His judgements upon His own are to bring us to a place of greater victory and alignment with His will and purposes. To those in captivity, Isaiah prophesied,

> *"Awake, awake!*
> *Put on your strength O Zion;*
> *Put on your beautiful garments,*
> *O Jerusalem, the holy city! . . .*
> *Shake yourself from the dust, arise;*
> *Sit down, O Jerusalem!*
> *Loose yourself from the bonds of your neck,*
> *O captive daughter of Zion!"*   (Isaiah 52:1–2)

We must choose to *arise* from our slumber and arise from the dust before we can *sit* in the place of authority with Him. Resting in the understanding of our delegated authority is prerequisite to loosing ourselves from those things that hold us captive. It's all a process!

Several years ago, I heard the story of a man in prison. One day he was released into the exercise yard for the first time and thought that because he was out of the confines of his little cell, he'd made it out of prison! What a rude shock he experienced to find that real freedom still eluded him. It is a bit like this in our Christian walk. We think that because we are *more* free than we used to be, we are really free. We have yet to discover the magnitude of the life God has for us outside of the prison walls!

The Lord has an inheritance for us but the only way we are going to apprehend it is with humility, an understanding of our desperate need for Him, and a determination to press into Him until we are over the wall of the prison yard! This entails, first and foremost, a willingness to be honest and let go of any self-deception about our spiritual condition as we come before the Lord and lay our hearts open before Him. My mother used to talk about "calling a spade a spade" when I was growing up. That's what we must be willing to do! Secondly, some action is required on our part. This action involves three verbs – *yielding* to, *trusting* and *obeying* the Lord as He leads us on. Getting over the wall of the prison yard is a process. The question I hear the Lord asking at this time is, "Are we willing to submit to that process?"

The chains upon our neck, the manacles upon our wrists and feet, even the walls of confinement around us are like paper – easily crushed by the sword of the Spirit and the shield of faith! However, they are nonetheless very real and are only removed *God's* way. He said His ways are not our ways (Isaiah 55:8–9). We know this intellectually, but we seem to live our lives as though God intends to do everything the way *we* would do it! In actuality, He has a way of doing things that He has ordained and we only experience His blessing when we approach things His way. Otherwise, our lives crumble around us and we are left trudging in endless circles like the Hebrews in the wilderness between Egypt and Canaan. It took them 40 years to make a journey of less than two weeks because they were stubborn, stiff-necked and expected things to happen their way. Moses missed out on the land of promise because he didn't do things God's way. He struck the rock when the Lord had instructed him to speak to the rock (compare Numbers 20:7–11 to Deuteronomy 32:48–52). David experienced tragedy because He did not bring up the Ark of the Covenant to Jerusalem the way God had said to do it (1 Chronicles 15:12–13). The Lord shows us the way in His Word and through the guidance of His Holy Spirit. His Word is a lamp to our feet, lighting the way (Psalm 119:105), and His Spirit guides us into all truth (John 16:13). These are His promises to us as we seek to yield ourselves to His will and His ways. We aren't left to grope our way through the darkness like blind men in a minefield! Rather, we have the promise of His leading as we place our hearts and lives into His hands.

This book shares some of the things the Lord has been showing me recently which I believe are important in this process of clambering over the prison wall into that wide expanse of free-dom and blessing, where His inheritance is *realized or actualized* in our lives. I've had such a cry in my heart to see God's people walking in what He purposed and ordained for us.

▶ *No matter where we are in Him, there is more! Whatever we have experienced, or seen, or touched or read about ... there is more! However much we have received of His nature and character, there is more!*

If you find a cry in your heart to trade your tattered and grubby prison clothes for His garments and mantle, then read on. If you have experienced a longing within to exchange your emptiness, weakness and bankruptcy for the wealth of His inheritance, then read on. This book is for you!

Prayer

Father, I admit that, to some degree at least, I have been in a place of self-delusion and captivity. I choose to put away childish things today and let go of any pretense, fantasy, or illusion in which I have lived regarding my relationship and my walk with You. I choose to embrace Your truth today, inviting Your Spirit of Truth to fill me and renew me. I confess that I am wretched, miserable, poor, blind and naked in so many ways. I recognize that You have so much more for me than what I have known or experienced. You have an abundance for me that is beyond what I could ask or even imagine! I am coming to You, Jesus, because You are my hope and my all in all. I am coming to You for Your refining fire and for Your righteousness. I so desperately need You and Your divine power to work in every area of my life. I'm weary of trying to do all the right things and yet making little progress. Lord, I need Your help to get over the prison wall. I have experienced Your healing and delivering power in my life, but there is still a long way to go! I desire to arise from the dust and loose myself from every bondage of the world, the flesh, and the kingdom of darkness in my life. I submit myself to You, Father, and to Your ways. Lead me by Your cords of love, dear Lord, as I submit my heart and life to You in a new and fresh way today. Amen.

Chapter 2

Coloring Outside the Lines

Proverbs 29:18 bluntly tells us, *"Where there is no vision, the people perish ..."* (KJV). Some translations read *"the people cast off restraint"*. Without His vision, the frame of reference that comes from God to redefine the world in *His* terms is missing! Other Old Testament passages say it in a little different way – that without an experiential knowledge of God and His kingdom, we remain in captivity or are destroyed (Isaiah 5:13; Hosea 4:6). An experiential knowledge of Him brings vision, the ability to see as He sees. It brings a new frame of reference, in terms of what is sin, but also in terms of what is possible in His kingdom. Our inability to see as He sees or to have His vision constitutes differing degrees of spiritual blindness. If we are spiritually blind, our understanding of reality is then hindered or limited by our blindness. We limit God to our own understanding of reality, putting Him in a box characterized by the dimensions of our own limitations.

▶ *Vision releases God from the box we have put Him in!*

His vision brings a new frame of reference that is not bound by the limitations of the physical world, the world system or our human thinking. Vision enables us to see the kingdom of God without these self-imposed limitations. It is seeing what God can do without watering things down by our inability to figure them out! Vision is seeing as God sees. There are *no* impossibilities (Luke 1:37; Matthew 17:20). There are *no* limitations! It is a fourth dimension that He calls His kingdom. His kingdom knows no end. It is timeless, immeasurable, indefinable, and indescribable! His kingdom is also called "eternity". The eternal life He came to bring to the world is part of this kingdom. Vision not only allows God out of the box we have put Him into, but having His vision enables us to climb out of the box into which we have put ourselves!

▶ *With His vision, our potential is no longer determined by who we are or what resources we have. Instead, our potential is determined by who God is and what resources He has!*

Jesus came to set us free from our spiritual blindness so that we can have His vision (Luke 4:18). Sometimes we think the spiritually blind are the people in the world who do not yet know Him. That is true. But the Church is not exempt from spiritual blindness! I am sad to report that some of most spiritually blind people I know are in the Church! The Apostle Paul said we only see dimly now, but there remains the promise of seeing and knowing in greater fullness (1 Corinthians 13:12). However, this increase in clarity need not wait until eternity. The Lord is showing me things all the time that I couldn't see before! He can do it for you!

Vision enables us to color outside the lines

There was a commercial on television in the United States a number of years ago that advertised four-wheel drive vehicles. The beginning of the ad showed young children coloring outside the lines in their coloring books. They were having a grand time coloring all over the page, unencumbered by any limitations imposed by publishers of the coloring books. The next scene depicted the same children as adults, still "coloring outside the lines" in their off-road vehicles! They were having a super time driving off the main roads where most people wouldn't dare to go.

Having God's vision enables us to color outside the lines in the sense that we are not limited to the pathways laid down by other human beings, past or present. We can dream the impossible dream, and watch it come to pass. We can break the mold to establish something new and different! With vision, we can dare to face floods, prisons, fiery furnaces, lion dens, giants, disease or hopeless situations with boldness and confidence because we know our Creator is still creating and calling into being those things which do not yet exist (Romans 4:17). We know He can change circumstances, create new hearts, cause obstacles to disappear, make provision out of nothing, and that the list goes on without end.

▶ *The extent to which we possess His vision determines how far we progress outside the "lines" or the boundaries of human logic, human reasoning, the world system or religious tradition.*

The story has been related about a bishop from the East Coast who visited a small, mid-western Christian college a number of years ago:

> "He stayed at the home of the college president, who also served as a professor of physics and chemistry. After dinner, the bishop declared that the millennium couldn't be far off, because just about everything about nature had been discovered and all inventions conceived. The young college president politely disagreed and said he felt there would be many more discoveries. When the angered bishop challenged the president to name just one such invention, the president replied he was certain that within fifty years men would be able to fly. 'Nonsense!' sputtered the outraged bishop. 'Only angels are intended to fly.' The bishop's name was Wright, and he had two boys at home who would prove to have greater vision than their father. Their names: Orville and Wilbur."[1]

Vision gives us a more complete picture

The extent to which we possess His vision determines how much of His kingdom we actually see and comprehend. Have you heard the story of the blind men and the elephant? Each one had hold of a different part of the elephant and was absolutely convinced that the elephant looked like the appendage they could feel. The one holding the trunk thought the elephant looked like a snake. The one with his hands on the elephant's leg was sure the elephant looked like a tree, and so forth. They actually argued over who was right. However, each man's concept of the elephant was incomplete. None of them had any idea how big the elephant really was or what it really looked like! The more of God's vision we have, the more we will be able to comprehend the utter vastness of His eternal kingdom. Paul prayed fervently for the Ephesian church this way:

> *"that He would grant you, according to the riches of His glory, to be strengthened with might through His Spirit in the inner man, that Christ may dwell in your hearts through faith; that you, being rooted and grounded in love, **may be able to comprehend with all the saints what is the width and length and depth and height – to know the love of Christ which passes knowledge; that you may be filled with all the fullness of God.**"* (Ephesians 3:16–19)

Paul was praying for them to have vision and for that vision to bring a more complete understanding of the infinite dimensions of the kingdom of God, of the love of Christ and the fullness of God with which we are to be filled. Most of us have hold of such a tiny part of God's vision for us. We have hold of the elephant's tail and think this is all there is!

Vision brings faith and hope

Without vision, we tend to be faithless and hopeless. The Bible helps us to see that without faith, it is impossible to please God (Hebrews 11:6), and that we are called to walk by faith and not by what we can see in the natural (2 Corinthians 5:7). I have found in my life that vision is one of the things that releases faith! The "hall of faith" in Hebrews 11 is filled with average people who by faith did extraordinary things. They were accurately identified by the author of the book of Hebrews as men and women of faith. But they were also men and women of vision! They had faith *because* they had a vision! They were able to envision something more than what was visible in the natural world. They could see beyond the way things appeared to the fulfillment of what God had said and what He had promised, even if it appeared to be an impossibility!

Vision gives us a view from the top

Ephesians 3:20 contains a mind blowing assertion! This verse tells us that, *"God is able to do exceedingly abundantly beyond all we could ask or think."* *Abundantly* literally means "without boundaries". God is able to do even more than this according to His Word. He is able to do *exceedingly* abundantly *beyond* all that we could ask or even *think*. If we can think it or imagine it, our vision is not big enough! His vision is bigger! Vision lifts us out of our human thinking and mindsets. It gives us a radical new perspective on things. It lifts us out of this worldly realm and gives us God's bird's-eye view from His throne and from the realm of eternity.

When I was 20 years old, I took my first trip west of the Mississippi River. I worked two jobs through the summer and saved enough to fly to Colorado and meet my boyfriend and his brothers there. We planned to drive through Colorado, Utah and Arizona to the Grand Canyon and then gradually make our way home through Texas and the Gulf coast states. First, however, we planned to backpack in a wilderness area close to where my friend, Steve, had been working in a summer job for the U.S. Forest Service. I had never seen mountains so big as the ones in Colorado! It took us days to hike up some of the peaks and we never did make it to the top. But we did make it above the tree line, where we had a panoramic view of Colorado for miles and miles. Everything looked so different from up there. Things that had looked so big on the ground were tiny little specks and that was if they were visible at all! There was a sense of freedom that accompanied the vision from that altitude that I had never experienced before as a flatlander from Georgia. I felt I could fly! It's like that when we get God's vision. Our perspective on everything changes, bringing fresh hope and new liberty.

Vision – a source of energizing

In our time in the northeast of England, we worked with a number of young people. We met kids who spent a good deal of their lives on street corners, drowning their pain and their boredom in alcohol and drugs. Some of these kids were only nine or ten years old. Most of them came from families that were both dysfunctional and impoverished. Many of these families had been on welfare or "the dole", as it is called in England, for successive generations. That was all these children had ever known. They expected to grow up and live off welfare too because they had no vision for anything more. All they could see were the bars of their economic prison and a lifetime of barrenness and monotony. Life was pointless and hopeless. They did not care about much of anything except keeping their supply of alcohol and cigarettes intact. They were already dying on the inside, even at such a young age. The Lord showed me they were perishing because they had no vision! At the time we left England to return to the United States, some of these young people were beginning to change. There was a new spark coming in their eyes. They were beginning to ask questions and were realizing that there was another world outside the box that they lived in. These kids captivated my heart. I pray for them daily, much the same way that the Apostle Paul prayed for the Ephesians. I pray that the eyes of their understanding would be enlightened and that they might *know* the hope of His calling (Ephesians 1:18). I pray for vision!

Vision is the spark that ignites a fire in our hearts. It ignites dormant passion, fuels motivation and energizes us to move forward in God. We don't have the "get up and go" to do any more than just survive each day if we have no vision. We don't have the energy to break new ground when there is a shortage of vision in our lives. We will not consider stretching beyond our comfort zones if there is no vision to motivate us!

▶ *Apathy, passivity and complacency are often the fruit of lack of vision.*

Being able to *see* something more than what we have stirs our hearts! There is a spiritual dynamic that takes place inside us when we have a vision.

The American pioneers pressed out into the wilderness of the New World to explore the unknown and settle those vast areas because they were people of vision. They were stirred by the accounts of this uncharted territory that could be theirs. They could see it so clearly in their mind's eye that they were willing to face hardship and even death to see the vision fulfilled. God has a land for us called His kingdom, and it remains largely uncharted. Allowing Him to give us a vision for it will lift us to new heights and life us to new levels! It will motivate and energize us, propelling us to a new place in Him!

Jeanne Guyon – a woman of vision

Jeanne Guyon (1648–1717) was a woman of vision. I read her classic, *Experiencing the Depths of Jesus Christ*,[2] during my time at Bible College. I was awed by her closeness to the Lord and the revelation she had of who He is and how He works. At that time, I knew only that she was a Frenchwoman in the Medieval Church. In researching another book, however, I found out much more about Madame Jeanne Guyon. Her life provides an amazing account!

As a young girl, Jeanne loved the Lord passionately and sought to bring glory to Him through her life. She studied the Bible fervently. She dispensed food to the poor, took the sick and suffering into her home, established hospitals, and weathered many tribulations, suffering mightily herself. She sought to walk through each tragedy, however, with grace and surrender to Jesus. Just as importantly, she wanted to share with others what she had found in Him.

▶   *Jeanne Guyon had a vision to see God's people step into a new place of intimacy in their relationship with Him.*

Widowed at a young age with three surviving children, she set out upon an apostolic journey through France and Switzerland to teach holiness based on faith and effective methods of prayer. This journey took eight years. Jeanne Guyon was loved and esteemed by those among whom she ministered. For this reason, she incurred the jealousy of the Church leaders at that time, who labeled her a heretic. She experienced horrendous persecution and imprisonment for seven years because of her religious beliefs, four of which were in the infamous Bastille. The last two years there she could receive no visitors, hold no conversations, and write no letters. In prison, she sang and wrote hymns, at least one of which is included in many modern hymnals. During her lifetime, she also authored forty books, including a twenty-volume commentary on the Bible.[3]

Jeanne Guyon found a place in God that was beyond anything in the natural world. She wrote, "We need not wait until tomorrow for the second coming of Christ, but we may see Him today, if we learn to still our inner selves." She taught that it is God Himself we need to seek, rather than His gifts. She shared that if we die to ourselves, we can receive His fullness. One of her hymns, translated into English by William Cowper, declares,

"To me remains nor place nor time:
My country is in every clime:
I can be calm and free from care
On any shore, since God is there."

How could a woman in seventeenth-century Europe, a widow with young children, travel through two nations as an apostle preaching and teaching to the multitudes? How could she write forty books? How could she weather such hardship and suffering with such joy and peace? Jeanne Guyon could accomplish such extraordinary feats because she was a woman of vision!

The mistake of settling for second-hand vision

When Dave and I were newlyweds, he tried to explain to me once about a house he envisioned. It was a house he dreamed of building at that time. The only thing I remember about this house is that it was octagonal! He talked to me about it for hours, and tried to describe it in detail for me because it was so clear in his mind. He even drew me diagrams of the house. I *wanted* to see it. I could *almost* see it. But I could never see it the way Dave could see it. If I were to then try to build this house, trying to act on Dave's vision, can you imagine what sort of trouble I would run into when it got down to the practical reality of building? I'd be lost! Dave could envision the completed house down to every last detail. All I could envision was a diagram of lines on a piece of paper. I would need to be able to see it with the same depth of clarity as Dave if I were to build successfully.

One problem we encounter as Christians is that we are often trying to walk in someone else's vision. It's the same as trying to walk in someone else's faith, someone else's authority or someone else's revelation. It doesn't work!

▶ *God's vision is something we must each possess for ourselves if we are going to learn to walk in our inheritance.*

It must be personal! The Lord has a vision for all of us as believers on three levels, and each can be very personal.

Firstly, He has a vision that is unique to us individually – what He wants to do *in* each of us and *through* each of us as individual believers. Secondly, He has a vision that is unique to a specific body or fellowship of believers, what He wants to do in them and through them corporately as a cell group or as a church. This is the level where we often stumble by settling for second-hand vision! In any group of Christians, the leaders usually have a vision. Many Christians will try to embrace the leaders' vision, but without really praying about it or trying to make it personal. The vision of the house can be put forward and held up by the leaders, but it should be personal to each member of that group as well! If God has planted us in a local body of believers, He has a reason for it. He has a plan. That plan will be intimately entwined with the corporate vision. I believe that if we pray and ask the Lord to give us His vision for that group, He will make the vision of the house ours. We will have ownership in it and He will show us what part we have to play in it individually. Finally, the Lord has for each of us a vision for the Body of Christ at large – what He wants to do in His people and through them around the world. If we are in tune with His mind and heart, we will generally have much the same vision for His Church as other believers. However, He will highlight specific things and emphasize the importance of different things in each of us so the vision He gives us will still be unique and personal. It's only as He makes His vision personal to us on all three levels that we can stand and pray with precision, boldness, and perseverance until we see His kingdom come on this earth as it is in heaven!

The book of James shows us that we do not have *because we do not ask* (James 4:2). If you feel that you are lacking a personal vision, either for yourself, your cell group or church, or for the Body of Christ at large, allow me to encourage you to *ask* the Lord to make His vision real in your heart. Jesus said that if we ask anything in His Name, the Father will give us what we have asked (John 14:13; 15:16; 16:23). "In His Name" entails asking according to His character and will (1 John 5:14–15). He desires that we have His vision even more than we desire it! We can ask Him for vision with confidence and excited anticipation. However, allow me to share a caution with you before you ask for His vision. Prepare to have your world turned upside down!

Prayer

Thank You for Your vision, Lord! Thank You that my life in You is not limited by what I can see, hear, taste, smell, feel, think, imagine or limited by what is normal, customary, or logical. Thank You that I am now, first and foremost, a citizen of the unseen world called the Kingdom of God and am now an heir of the riches of this Kingdom. Thank You for new revelation! I invite You to open my eyes, Lord. Thank You for healing my blindness and helping me to see this Kingdom and see You as I have never seen You before! I pray You will give me the courage to climb to the mountaintop with You to gain Your perspective on the world around me. I also ask for courage to color outside the lines, to walk where no man has walked before, to break the mold of tradition to follow Your heart and Your leading. Help me, dear Lord, to let You out of the box into which I have relegated You. Please forgive me for limiting You to what I have been able understand. As I receive Your forgiveness and Your cleansing today, I ask boldly for Your vision! I want to be a spiritual pioneer, walking where I have never walked before, discovering and exploring Your kingdom in a fresh way. I pray that You will anoint my eyes to *see* the vastness of Your kingdom, but also that You would grace me, dear Lord, to step out in faith to *walk* in it. Amen.

Notes

1. Craig Brian Larson (ed.), *Illustrations for Preaching and Teaching* (Baker Books, Grand Rapids, 1993), p. 261.
2. Madame Jeanne Guyon, *Experiencing the Depths of Jesus Christ* (reprinted by Christian Books, Goleta, CA).
3. Edith Deen, *Great Women of the Christian Faith* (Barbour and Company, Uhrichsville, Ohio, 1959), pp. 130–140.

Chapter 3

It's All About Being, Not Doing!

My husband, Dave, and I worked closely with a large Christian organization a number of years ago. It was a difficult time for us because we were all too busy working for God to build close relationships. The emphasis was on building His kingdom, so everyone pushed hard to achieve more. Very little time was devoted to relaxation, reflection or getting to know one another. I cannot say that I have been completely liberated from working too hard in the ministry or that I have learned to allow as much time as is needed for relationship building. The Lord is still working with me in these matters! I have, however, come to see a few things more clearly in the ensuing years. It is increasingly apparent to me that "working for God" is a subtle trap into which much of the Church world has fallen. I see a snare of the enemy in this kind of thinking that holds many of God's people captive. Yet it *seems* so good, so religious, *so biblical*! How can this be?

Our adversary is very good at taking the Word of God and using it to tempt us into a trap of his own insidious design. Look at what happened during Jesus' forty days in the wilderness. Satan used his thousands of years of experience in tripping up humankind to try to stop Jesus and thwart His mission. What did the devil use? He used the Scriptures! In the same way, he will try to ensnare us in his web by using the Scriptures, along with logic that sounds very good and very biblical! That is why it is so important that we know the *full* counsel of God revealed in Genesis through Revelation, and have a personal experiential understanding of His mind, heart, will and purposes for us. These things are not gleaned through the Scriptures alone, but rather through an intimate relationship with the Lord. Jesus told the Pharisees that they searched the Scriptures thinking that in them was eternal life, but the life is *in Him* and they would not come to Him (John 5:39). So many of us are sidetracked and even shipwrecked through a faulty interpretation of the Word of God because we are well versed in the letter of the Law but don't know the Spirit behind it. We go to the written Word, but we don't go to Jesus who is the Living Word. We've learned all *about* Him, but we do not know Him. We don't know God's heart!

The Father's desire for a family

What is the Father's heart when it comes to His children? Why did He create us in the first place? A key may be found in Genesis 2 where we find that God breathed the very breath of Himself, all that He is, into Adam giving him life (Genesis 2:7). Then God told Adam it was not good for man to be alone (Genesis 2:18). Humanity, the Hebrew word *'adam*, was created in God's image. Like the image stamped on a coin, mankind was created to show the nature and attributes of God. This was all marred by the fall, of course, with that image being shattered and cracked so that the likeness was no longer true to the original. It's interesting that when God looked over all that He had created, He determined that *"it was very good"* (Genesis 1:31). And yet there was one thing in all His creation that He lamented that was "not good" – that this man *made in His own image* was alone (Genesis 2:18). Is there a clue here? Was the Creator's purpose in creating a race of beings that were *like Him* to provide for Himself a bride and a family because it was not good that *He* was alone?

A study of the Scriptures, both Old and New Testaments, seems to suggest such a purpose. A desire to meet with His people can be seen throughout the Old Testament. He met with Moses face to face (Exodus 33:11). He called the tabernacle the "tent of meeting" because it was the place He designed and set apart for His priests to meet with Him. His very presence came and dwelt between the wings of the cherubim on the Ark of the Covenant so that He could be with His people. Through the major prophets of the Old Testament He spoke of His people as if they were married to Him, referring to Himself as their "husband" and calling their idolatry "adultery" (see for example

Jeremiah 3:8–10, 14, 19–22; 13:27; Isaiah 54:6; 62:5; Ezekiel 6:9; 16:31–32; Hosea 3:1). He also spoke of Judah and Israel as His children and referred to Himself as their "Father" (Isaiah 63:16; 64:8; Jeremiah 31:9; Malachi 1:6). Most of us are probably more familiar with the New Testament. There, He calls His redeemed people His "bride". But He also calls us His "children", and "sons" who are co-heirs with Christ of His rich inheritance. The Creator, Jehovah, also refers to Himself as "Father" in the New Testament. There is an emphasis on communion with Him and on knowing Him intimately. It is apparent from the Scriptures that He created us *because He wants to be with us!*

The only thing that separates us from Him is our carnal, sinful nature. His remedy for this condition is to conform us to the image of His Son (Romans 8:29). In other words, His desire is that we become more and more like Him, increasingly restored back into the image of God as He works His process of salvation in our lives. The more like Him we become, the more intimacy we can experience with Him because the relationship is not marred by sin. Subsequently, His passion is centered on who we are and who we are becoming, *not* what we can do for Him!

Being who we were created to be

The Word, especially the New Testament, is full of references to who God created us to be. This is our true identity. To understand our true identity, we need only look at God's nature and character to see what He created us to be in His image. That identity was lost at the fall when Adam came under the control and dominion of Satan, and then begat sons in his own fallen image (Genesis 5:3). Now, however, through Jesus Christ, our true identities can be released and the image of God restored in us as we embrace His salvation and the work of His Spirit in our lives. This is the process of sanctification and ultimately the process of transformation! This Christian walk is, in many ways, the process of self-discovery that eluded us for so long as unbelievers.

I remember agonizing through my college days, wondering, "Who am I? Why do I exist?" People used to say back then that young people were searching "to find themselves". Many of us never did. I believe this has to do in part with the fact that we cannot – apart from knowing the One who made us because we were made in His image!

▶ *In knowing Him, we can finally come to know ourselves.*

Not the fallen, captive, blind, deluded, confused, carnal self, but rather the "real me" that each of us were created to be!

The more I have walked with the Lord, the more I have become convinced that maturity grows out of being rather than doing. God said He is looking for sons led by His Spirit whose character has been formed by the process of His work in their lives (Romans 8:14; Hebrews 12:7–8). The Greek word usually translated "son" is the word *huios*. It can be distinguished from the other words used for God's children in that it alone refers to those with knowledge, those who have already apprenticed and are ready to take their place alongside their Father in his business. They can be entrusted with His business because they are mature, stable, and know their Father's mind and desires. They are ready to have their name painted on the heavenly sign that says, "Creator & Son".

▶ *Sadly, even though God is looking for **sons**, what we usually offer Him are **employees**.*

He desires a relationship but, instead, we give Him a good job. He is looking at who we are becoming as any proud father would, and we are busily trying to make up for the lack in that area by pointing out what we are doing!

Looking for what we need in all the wrong places

We often say that our flurry of activity in Church work or ministry is "for the Lord". But is it? I think most of the time our motives are mixed. Of course we love Him and want to please Him. However, we often have other motives which center around:

• Living up to what we think are His expectations or the expectations of the Church.

• Finding our value and self-worth in recognition or achievement.

- Looking for our security in the acceptance and approval of other people.

A good test to see if this applies is to ask yourself the following questions: "If I could do absolutely nothing for God, would I feel unworthy or worthless? Would I feel like a nobody?" If our answer is "yes" to those questions, then we are probably looking for our value, self-worth and identity in what we do. However, our Father wants us to find these things in our relationship to Him – in *who we are!*

I learned this lesson with difficulty a number of years ago. In our first pastorate, I was known as Pastor Dee. It was always Pastor Dee this and Pastor Dee that. Not recognizing the enemy's trap, I began to increasingly find my identity in being a pastor. I began to confuse who I was with what I was doing. My identity and my value were in ministry and how hard I was working for God as Pastor Dee. You can guess what happened when the Lord told us to turn the church over to another couple, and move to another state with no initial direction about what He wanted us to do there! We knew we had heard from God so we obediently released the church, moved to the new place and waited on the Lord for His plan to unfold. It was agony, however, because I didn't know who I was anymore! No longer Pastor Dee, I felt as though I had lost my anchor. The truth was that Jesus had always wanted to be my anchor, but I had allowed it to be my ministry instead.

▶ *What we do will change with time, but who we are in Him will never change.*

Through all of this I experienced a rude awakening which was difficult and painful to work through. However, the Father allowed it to expose the snare of the enemy and to restore me to the place of a son where I could focus on my relationship with Him once again.

I question the wisdom of the recent emphasis on titles in the Body of Christ. At every turn, I encounter some promotion of Apostle John, Prophetess Betty or Evangelist Phil. Aside from the fact that it seems contrary to what God is doing in our midst in this hour to break down the barriers between leaders and laity and to release the entire Body into ministry, I believe it puts an unhealthy emphasis on titles and position. This trend reinforces the popular misconceptions that unless one has been given a title or position one is not qualified to lead or minister, and that our identity is determined by our function in the Body of Christ. Jesus warned against this, using the Pharisees as an example. He said they loved to be referred to by their title "Rabbi", but went on to tell the multitudes and his disciples not to fall into this same trap *"for you are all brethren"* (Matthew 23:1–8).

To continue testing the motives behind our activity, we could further ask ourselves the questions: "Would I find it inordinately disturbing if my hard work did not earn the acceptance and approval of my boss or pastor or mentor or congregation? Would I change what I was doing to gain their approval?" If the answer is "yes", then we may be looking for security in the acceptance and approval of others. Our Father wants us to find our security in *who we are* as His kids, His bride, the ones He died for!

We once worked with a gentleman who was desperate to please the man of God who had mentored him for a number of years. He felt he owed this man so much and wanted to serve this man and his ministry, to give back to him something of what he had received from him. It was also very important to have this older man's approval and blessing. In fact, our associate had a favored status with his mentor, being welcomed into his family and treated like a son. This status satisfied his rather acute need for security, but he was driven to work even harder to achieve things that would honor and please this man to keep the security intact. More and more, our friend seemed to find himself caught up in a need to perform because he was trying to find his security in the wrong place.

Burnout and bankruptcy

It's not that the Lord does not want us to do anything, but it is *out of relationship with Him* that the doing should flow! He wants us to be tied in so tightly with Him that He can guide and direct our activity. Without this kind of rooting and grounding in Him, burnout and spiritual bankruptcy lie just around the corner.

We became friends with a denominational minister at one point in our ministry. The more we got to know him, the more evident it became that he viewed his pastorate as a job not a calling. It was the job that seemed to hold his focus, not his relationship with the Lord or what God wanted to do in him. Though his enthusiasm had become miniscule and his heart was not in it, he stayed in the position and continued to do the work. The strain eventually took its toll. He hit the place of burnout and his life seemed to fall apart. He left his wife for a much younger woman. He not only left the ministry but, in his weakened state, began involving himself in things that would exact an even greater toll on his spiritual health and well-being. It was all very sad.

I believe, however, that if we are discerning and our hearts open to the Lord, we can make the necessary changes in our lives *before* a crash comes. He will try to get our attention and intervene, exposing where we have fallen into the trap of focusing on what we are doing instead of who we are becoming. He will show us the unhealthy patterns in our lives that inevitably lead to a bankruptcy of spirit, if we will only listen!

Breaking the unhealthy cycles

Seeking to meet our needs through service or ministry, our place in the church, or through the recognition that comes through titles or positions, will eventually leave us bereft and empty of spiritual life and power. The void in our lives then keeps us holding onto these things all the more so that emptiness will not be exposed. It is a vicious circle! When our focus is on doing things for Him or trying to keep our niche in the kingdom intact, intimacy with the Lord becomes more and more a thing of the past. Increasingly, we operate out of our own strength not His. We begin to operate more out of the flesh than the Spirit. We are replenished less and less by Him, as the level in our spiritual fuel tank steadily decreases, until eventually we are running on empty and we know it. We then do even more and hold even tighter onto the things we are substituting for Him, so that no one will see how empty we are! Does this sound familiar?

In reflecting on such circular hazards, the Apostle Paul's anguished cry at the end of Romans 7 comes to mind. *"Who will set me free from this body of death?"* he asked. Paul was entrapped in a vicious cycle himself. The answer comes in the next few verses at the beginning of Romans 8. The Spirit of life in Christ Jesus sets each of us free from the law of sin and death working in our lives. We need only stop and embrace His Spirit of life! We need only stop and embrace He who is the Way, the Truth and *the Life*. Jesus said He came to bring us abundant life. The picture He paints is that of life overflowing, uncontainable, and without boundaries. Yet we don't find it or experience it because we are so busy doing!

▶ *Our busyness acts as a barrier to block us from intimacy with the Lord and from receiving His life, His transforming power and His anointing.*

It keeps us locked into a cycle of emptiness, powerlessness and quiet desperation. That is until we recognize our need and do something about it!

I heard many years ago something that Kathryn Kuhlman had said, which really impacted my spirit at the time. Periodically, the Lord gives me a nudge and challenges me with it again. He continues to hold it up to me like a beacon, stirring me to press on to a higher place of His anointing and power. The statement I remember went like this, "Anyone can have the anointing if they are willing to pay the price." The price is time in His presence, becoming more like Him as we behold His glory (2 Corinthians 3:18). Are we willing to pay the price? Mary faced this choice in Luke 10 when Jesus was visiting the home she shared with her brother, Lazarus, and her sister, Martha. Despite Martha's resentment that Mary was not doing more, Mary opted to sit at Jesus' feet as a disciple. She chose to allow His glory to transform her and His words to impart life to her spirit as she utilized the opportunity to press closer to Him. She chose becoming over doing! Jesus told Martha, who did not under-stand, that Mary had chosen the higher way. Which way will we choose?

Allowing God to "fashion" us

When Jesus called His disciples, He said to them, *"Follow Me, and I will make you fishers of men"* (Matthew 4:19). There is a making process that the Lord wants to accomplish in each of our lives.

He did not tell His disciples, "If you follow Me I will send you out to *do* much fishing for Me." No, it was rather, "I will *make you fishermen.*" The Greek word used is one that means to construct, form, fashion or be the author of (as in "creator"). It engenders the picture of God fashioning us to *be* first and foremost, not launching us to *do.* My husband, a wonderful fisherman of many years, will attest to the fact that there is a great deal of difference in being a fisherman and one who fishes! I fish. I can use a fly rod and I know how to cast. Usually I enjoy it and sometimes I even catch a fish! But Dave is a real fisherman. He doesn't just fish; it is a part of who He is. This is also why his worship leading is so anointed. He doesn't just play music or lead worship; it is a part of who He is. Jesus *has made him* a worshiper! The doing will flow out of the being, if we will just get the being right first! What is God making you into? What sort of pot is the Potter fashioning? Who are you, really? I pray that you will take time to find out as you consider that being, not doing, is what it is all about!

Prayer

Father, I have been caught up in the trap of trying to find value, recognition and perhaps even my identity in what I can *do* for You. I have settled for being an employee rather a son. I've missed Your best as the relationship with You took a backseat to all that I have been doing for You or for others. Father, please forgive me for my blindness. I thought I was doing what was good and right in Your eyes. I now see that I have been deceived and fallen into the enemy's trap. Please cleanse me from all unrighteousness according to 1 John 1:9 as I confess my sin to You. Father, I also ask You to cleanse me from any idolatry that causes me to look to other things to fulfill me and satisfy the emptiness within. I invite You to cleanse me from all pride, and from the shame and fear that would keep me in the vicious cycle of working and doing to cover up my sense of inadequacy and failure. Please restore me by the power of your Spirit to a deeper relationship of intimacy with You. Lord, I need an impartation of Your strength and boldness to put that relationship with You first and stand against all the other things pulling on me and clamoring for my time and attention. Help me to walk in a place of balance, keeping my eyes fixed firmly on You. Help me to see who You have created me to be and who You want me to become. Help me to rest in my identity as Your child, Your heir, and Your bride. Help me to rest in who You are in me, so that out of my oneness with You can flow the gifts, the callings, the ministries and the service that is part of Your plan and purpose for my life. Amen.

Chapter 4

Fruit Trees or Christmas Trees?

Recently, I received the news that a well-known pastor had just confessed to his church about an affair he had been having with a staff member of the same sex. This man had built up a very large ministry and had a huge following. Though he had created a polished image on the outside, he apparently still had unresolved issues on the inside that could not stand up to the pressure of a growing ministry. He was great at building things for God but had somehow missed God building things in Him. He was bold and confident, knew His Bible, and could hear from the Lord. Yet there was a fatal flaw that led him into a lifestyle of deception, perversion, and self-gratification. Perhaps I was not as surprised as some when the news came out, but it shook me nonetheless. I was grieved that this man could make it so far without anyone recognizing the bankruptcy of spirit existing underneath his glossy and self-assured image. My heart bleeds for him because he probably has no idea what went wrong! He is another casualty of a Church system that encourages people to focus on looking good to the detriment of being rooted and grounded in the Lord.

Larry Crabb wrote a book a number of years ago called *Inside Out*.[1] The theme of the book was that real change can happen in our lives if we are willing to allow God to work from the inside out. However, we try to do it all backwards. We want to clean up the outside and get it looking good first! Many times all our doing, doing, doing is a part of this attempt to look good and be well thought of. But while we are so busy polishing the outside of our vessel and making it look good, the inside is full of corruption, lies we are believing about ourselves, God and other people and a host of other rubbish. Why did Jesus call the Pharisees "white-washed sepulchers"? It was because they were quite willing to let the inside stay full of dead things as long as the outside looked good!

The choice we are all given

In the first few years of our ministry in England, there were a number of young people saved from the surrounding community. We began to nurture them in their walk with the Lord. I became the youth leader and traveled with these teenagers to various youth events, seminars and camps. At one point, Dave and I became very burdened and grieved over how carnal the kids were and how closely they were straddling the fence with one foot in the world and one in the Church. This was despite the incredibly wonderful, awesome and anointed teaching they were receiving! When we were with other youth groups we found ourselves embarrassed by our group's rough edges. We began to compare them to the kids in these other youth groups, thinking the others looked so "Christian" and ours still looked like a group of kids off the street. Then the Lord pulled us up one day and said to us, "You have a choice here. You can easily make the kids into Christmas trees that simply look pretty because they will *want* to look good in order to please you. However, if you allow that to happen, they will only look good on the outside. They will have no real root in Me from which to grow. They'll be like a cut tree in a bucket that can only keep up appearances for so long. They will have colorful lights and pretty baubles on the outside, but they will not have much life on the inside. Alternatively, you can let *Me* grow fruit trees. You can let *Me* do the work in them *My* way in *My* timing. It will take a lot longer and they will look undeveloped, straggly and messy for a long time. But in the end, it will be *My* life that sustains them and the results will be lasting. Now which do you want?" Of course, we chose fruit trees! We *all* face the same choice in our walk with the Lord. Do we want to be Christmas trees or fruit trees?

Called to bear fruit

Jesus said in John 15:16,

> *"You did not choose Me, but I chose you and appointed you that you should go and bear fruit, and that your fruit should remain."*

We are called to bear fruit in our Christian walk. It is His plan and purpose for us. It is our destiny! So often in the Church world, however, when I hear people speak of fruit, what they are talking about is works. In our human way of thinking, we tend to equate fruit with accomplishment and achievement. I think God's perspective on it is a little different. There is a list of the fruit He desires to see manifest in our lives in Galatians 5:22–23. He is looking for the fruit of His Spirit in our lives: love, joy, peace, longsuffering, kindness, goodness, faithfulness, gentleness, and self-control. These words don't seem to describe anything beyond the ordinary until we start studying what each really means. Then we discover that they encompass a complete character change, even for those who have always been "good" people!

▶ *God wants to radically save us and radically change us!*

However, it only happens as we allow Him to do a deep work of transformation in our hearts, making us more and more like Him.

Christ becoming our life

The Bible College Dave and I attended in the 1980s emphasized knowing Jesus Christ by revelation and allowing Him to become our very life. The importance of sanctification and holiness was stressed, but as a work of the Spirit in the inner man not as an affectation in dress or appearance. I remember the founder of the college weeping over us and pleading with us, "Don't leave this place until you know Him and until He has become your life." I cannot help but wish that the pastor who recently confessed his homosexual affair had had the opportunity to train for ministry in such a place. The Apostle Paul told the Galatian church,

"I have been crucified with Christ; it is no longer I who live, but Christ lives in me."   (Galatians 2:20)

This passage became very familiar to Dave and me during those years of Bible College. The process of allowing our carnal nature to be crucified is not complete in either one of us, but that process has become a part of who we are as Christ is increasingly becoming our life!

The Holy Spirit has continued our education through the years. We've broadened in our approach to ministry as the Lord has sharpened some of the tools in our tool belts and as we have drawn from different streams. However, the one thing that has stayed constant is an absolute conviction that an intimate relationship with the Lord and a heart willing to yield, trust and obey are the keys to maturity and stability in our Christian walk. If anything, I think our understanding of their importance has actually *increased* the longer we have pastored and counseled. We've realized that we can counsel until we are blue in the face. We can do spiritual warfare all day long. And we can prophesy over people and speak things into their lives that do bring *a measure* of life and freedom. In the end, however, what really matters are the choices people make and their willingness to press into God and take responsibility in their relationship with Him. It all depends on how badly we want Him!

A willingness to surrender

I had close contact with a woman for several years who really struggled with taking personal responsibility in her walk with God. Outwardly, she was a very dignified woman who had been around the Church world for a long time. She seemed to really love the Lord. She had many gifts and the Lord had obviously deposited a great deal in her through the years. I could see what He wanted to do in and through her to touch others with His love and grace. That made it all the more grievous because I never saw her come close to a place where He *could* release her. She never gave Him enough of herself to allow Him to do it. Every time I saw her or spoke with her, she would lament about the battle she was in. She continued to go around the same mountain over and over again because she could never surrender fully to Him in the areas in which He was dealing with her heart. As a consequence her normal pattern was flight, usually to a new church, when things heated up inside her. Nothing was ever resolved or settled. The last I heard, she had moved on to yet another church to go around the mountain another time. My heart was broken for her because she really believed that other people were to blame for the emptiness in her life. She was so desperate for more of what she knew God had for her, yet could not see that the real barrier lay within.

I would like to share a lovely contrast, however. In a recent Alpha course that I was helping to lead, there was a young Muslim man who was asking for any books to read about Christianity that I thought might be helpful to him. I gave Kamal a book that had been recommended to me entitled *I Dared to Call Him Father* by Bilquis Sheikh.[2] Before I gave him the book, I read it to see if it would be suitable for him. My heart was really touched by the author's testimony. In fact, at times I was moved to tears! As a brand new believer in Pakistan, she was so sensitive to the voice of the Lord and to His presence, allowing Him to guide her daily actions and speech in a way that was very precious. Every day He gently corrected, guided and loved her into His image. I felt the Lord challenging *me* to be as sensitive to His leading as this new believer! It was not legalism or religiosity or a formula that was operating in her life, but holiness that came as the result of a simple desire to be in the Lord's presence and be obedient to Him. As proud and imperious as her natural man was, she wanted God so badly that she was willing to surrender and yield to Him constantly without putting up the resistance that we usually think of as "normal".

The problem with formulae

So often in the Church world we are looking for formulae to bring instant change to our lives and situations. I believe this constant search for a formula keeps us from finding the place of simple desire for God and obedience that Bilquis Sheikh had discovered.

I had a number of friends in the 1980s who immersed themselves in a particular Christian movement. While I recognized the truth in the movement's message, I saw and heard some things that I felt missed the mark of God's best. One thing I noticed was that my friends seemed to look to the written Word of God as a band-aid type formula to apply to any situation. It was easier for them to pull a promise out of the Word to confess and stand on than it was to go to the Lord and find out His mind, heart and will for a particular person or situation. I noticed that they knew the Bible very well, but didn't appear to know Jesus so well. I was reminded of Jesus' words to the religious people of His day when He lamented how they searched the Scriptures for what they were seeking, yet didn't come to Him for it (John 5:39–40). It is always easier to look for a formula than to make the effort to press into God! Formulas end up being a substitute for relationship.

▶ *However, real faith flows out of our relationship with the Lord, not out of our skill in applying a formula.*

Another thing I noticed was that this group of friends didn't have a lot of staying power. They wanted their circumstances to change quickly. Spiritual principles like perseverance, tenacity, and endurance were not things they talked about much. Neither was the Cross. Perhaps they hadn't come to know God well enough at that point to understand how He works. He often uses painful and difficult situations in our lives to bring us to the end of ourselves, build character and put us on the road to maturity. My friends were rooted and grounded in the written Word, but not rooted and grounded in the living Word – the person of Jesus Christ.

The price of fruit trees

One of my greatest frustrations and sorrows as a pastor could be expressed in the old adage, "You can lead a horse to water but you can't make him drink!" So often we can see that people are busy polishing up the outside while the inside rots away, or that they are rootless in terms of their personal relationship with the Lord. But as much as we teach, counsel, pray for people and try to lead by example, it is still up to the individual to count the cost and pay the price of intimate relationship. Unfortunately, many are not willing to pay that price. Like the rich ruler (Luke

18), who came to Jesus and asked, *"What must I do to inherit eternal life?"* most of us are saddened by the thought of giving up anything. We blithely pray, "Thy kingdom come, thy will be done on earth as it is in heaven," not realizing what it will cost us to see that prayer answered!

▶ *The salvation is free but it costs us everything to apprehend and actualize the inheritance He has for us.*

When there is an inheritance to be had, it is because someone has died. I used to teach that God paid the price for us to have His inheritance by dying Himself. That is true. But just recently the Lord has shown me more. He has quickened to my spirit in a fresh way that *we must also die* to receive His inheritance! It is only secured when we are willing to give up our lives for His. As Jesus told His disciples,

> *"For whoever desires to save his life will lose it, but whoever loses his life for My sake will find it."*   (Matthew 16:25)

It is through this death-to-self process that we truly find and walk in the riches of God's inheritance for His children.

In some ways, the parable of the prodigal son illustrates this process. It is not just a story about backsliders! Judson Cornwall wrote a thought-provoking little book in 1979 called *Give Me Make Me*[3] with new revelation and fresh insight into this well-known parable. He used the young man's two requests, *"give me"* (Luke 15:12) and *"make me"* (Luke 15:19) to illustrate the two attitudes with which we can approach our Father. He follows the son's life through the hardships he experienced, and shows how growth and maturity followed as a result. The young man grew from a place of selfishness, simply wanting the inheritance and blessing of his father (give me), to a state where all he longed for was the relationship with his father to be renewed and to be made into one worthy of sonship (make me). It took ruin and hitting rock bottom before this could happen. It also took a repentant and humble heart to come back to the father, confessing his unworthiness and his failure, for him to experience *"beauty for ashes and the oil of joy for mourning"* (Isaiah 61:3). It takes coming to the end of ourselves before God can take our failings and our mistakes and turn them for good in our lives!

▶ *It is through the death-to-self process that God makes us into fruit trees.*

Near where we once lived in New Mexico, there is a valley famous for its juicy apples. A native of the area once told me that the trees that produce the tastiest apples are the ones that have been through the hardest winters. Can you see the spiritual parallel? Psalm 66:10–12 says this:

"For You, O God, have tested us;
You have refined us as silver is refined.
You brought us into the net;
You laid affliction on our backs.
You have caused men to ride over our heads;
We went through fire and through water;
But You brought us out to rich fulfillment."

There is a spiritual richness and wealth that comes into our lives as a result of those trials and hardships that bring us to the end of ourselves. That wealth is His life in us, filling us, infusing us, and coursing through our veins! We can choose to run away from the hardships, frustrations and pressures. Or we can embrace them with a yielded heart and an understanding of the process of God and how He works His nature and character into our lives. My mother-in-law has a cute needlework picture hanging in one bathroom. It says, "It takes both sunshine and rain to make a rainbow!" God uses both the good times and the bad to make our lives a thing of His beauty.

L.B. Cowan was a missionary in China who understood the value of hardship. She wrote in her well-known devotional, *Streams in the Desert*:

"Toys and trinkets are easily earned, but the most valuable things carry a heavy price. The highest places of power are always bought with blood, and you can attain those pinnacles if you have enough blood to pay. That is the condition of conquering the holy heights everywhere. The story of true heroics is always the story of sacrificial blood. The greatest values and character in life are not blown randomly across our path by wayward winds, for great souls experience great sorrows."[4]

We pay in blood but reap a treasure beyond valuation as we submit to the Lord's process in our lives. It is worth the price!

A dear friend with an extremely debilitating disease was sharing with me at one point that she had come to a place of utter desperation. I felt so helpless and at such a loss for any life-giving words of encouragement or comfort. I knew that if I were in her position, I would probably be feeling similarly desperate! I quietly whispered to the Lord, "Help! I don't know how to encourage her!" He just as quietly whispered back to me, "Tell her that the point of desperation can be the end . . . or it can be the beginning." Desperation can be the doorway to hopelessness and emptiness, or it can be the doorway to discovering new depths of His life and empowerment. We get to choose!

When we choose to embrace the hardships and allow our desperation to be the beginning of a new step in God, we pay a price as we withstand the wind, the storms, the isolation and cold. However, the result is that our roots go down deep into the soil of the Divine! Moreover, we are not easily shaken or blown over by the next winter season we go through. Our roots in Him make us stable and secure. These roots also tap us into the limitless riches and resources of His kingdom, so that everything He is can now become a part of who we are!

Prayer

Lord, I confess to You that I have been working hard to polish up the outside while allowing things that grieve Your heart to remain on the inside. I have been more concerned with what other people see than with what You see. I ask Your forgiveness, Lord. Please forgive me and cleanse me of everything that would defile this temple. I ask You to do a *deep* work in me. I want to surrender to You in a more complete way than I ever have before. Help me to be willing to pay the price. Help me to be sensitive to Your voice as You show me the way to walk. Help me to turn every place of hardness in My heart over to You. I ask You to take my heart of stone and give me a soft, supple, yielded heart. Lord, I ask You to plant new desires in My heart, a new desire for You that will cause me to want You so badly that I will be willing to give my life for Yours. Help me to embrace the hardships and trials that You allow into My life. Lord, I want my roots to go down deep in You. I choose today to be a fruit tree not a Christmas tree! As I make this choice, I ask You to make me into the person You have purposed me to be. Amen.

Notes

1. Larry Crabb, *Inside Out* (NavPress, Colorado Springs, 1988).
2. Bilquis Sheikh, *I Dared to Call Him Father* (Kingsway Publications, Eastbourne, 1978).
3. Judson Cornwall, *Give Me Make Me* (Logos International, Plainfield, NJ, 1979).
4. L.B. Cowan (ed. James Reimann), *Streams in the Desert* (Zondervan, Grand Rapids, 1997; first copyright 1925), p. 414.

Chapter 5

Avoiding
the Sinkhole Syndrome

Growing up in the American state of Georgia as a teenager, I read a story in the Atlanta newspaper one day about a sinkhole that had opened up in Florida very close to where a childhood friend of mine lived. It was about fifty feet across and had swallowed up a car. They were concerned it was going to suck a nearby house down into its depths as well. Imagine sitting quietly in your house reading a book and then, without warning, plunging into the depths of some bottomless hole never to be seen again! I was amazed. I didn't think such shocking things happened in real life! The sinkhole was apparently caused by the gradual decrease of water in an underground river or aquifer under the area in question. The result was a massive cave-in of earth into the void created by the loss of the underground water. I have since heard of other sinkholes occurring in various places. I've concluded they must be more common than I had originally thought.

I have also concluded that spiritual sinkholes are common in the lives of Christians! As ministers and counselors, we see many people who seem to go through life experiencing one sinkhole after another. There is a massive spiritual and emotional cave-in as they lose touch with the river of God inside of them. Some Christians have never been in touch with this river at all. They have lived for years trying to make it on their own steam, never knowing that there was a river of living water available to them through the Holy Spirit.

The river of God

Psalm 46:4 (NIV) says,

> *"There is a river whose streams make glad the city of God,*
> *the holy place where the Most High dwells."*

The holy place where He dwells is now in us! As the Apostle Paul described it, our bodies are temples of the Holy Spirit and we are His dwelling place (1 Corinthians 3:16; Romans 8:9). Speaking of the presence of the Holy Spirit who would come to dwell within those who believe, Jesus said that out of our innermost beings would flow rivers of living water (John 7:38). These rivers of the Spirit water our own hearts and lives, as well as those of others as we make ourselves available to the Lord to be vessels through whom His life can flow. Psalm 1 speaks of the one whose delight is in the Lord as being like a tree planted by a river:

> *"He shall be like a tree*
> *Planted by the rivers of water,*
> *That brings forth its fruit in its season,*
> *Whose leaf also shall not wither;*
> *And whatever he does shall prosper."*   (Psalm 1:3)

Part of God's process of making us fruit trees is to establish us in a place of abiding by the river of His Spirit. As we allow ourselves to be planted and established by the Lord, we see fruitfulness and spiritual prosperity in our lives.

A cave-in happens when we never reach or somehow lose touch with this river. The river is the teeming stream of His life and presence within us. It is in His presence where we find spiritual refreshing (Acts 3:19) and where our strength is renewed as we wait upon Him (Isaiah 40:31). As we allow the river of His Spirit to water our own spirits, we find our inner man being renewed day by day (2 Corinthians 4:16). When we don't, sinkholes are the result! Many of us recognize the sinkholes in our lives. We see clearly the bankruptcy and the emptiness that lead to the development of these sinkholes. However, we can acknowledge the need without ever doing anything about it.

A close call!

One January a few years ago, the Lord began to warn me to press in closer to Him and wait upon Him more fully. I knew I was not where I needed to be in my relationship with Him. I'd let other things crowd in and I was beginning to slip into doing things more in my own strength. I said "yes" to Him, but then never really did anything about it. Subsequently, Dave and I found ourselves in a situation with a house that we were buying that brought me to a place of despair. We knew the Lord had said this was the house He wanted us to buy, but we really had to fight for it! Everything that could go wrong in the deal seemed to go wrong. Everywhere we turned there was a blockage. Every step of the way we were going back to the Lord and asking Him if we had heard Him correctly. After months of torment, we wanted desperately to give up and go back to a normal life. But the Lord kept saying "no" and compelling us to press on. It was such a long and arduous trial over many months that I was left empty, dry and at the end of my tether. This point was reached long before the last obstacle was cleared in September! I realized through this situation how much more I needed to be abiding in Him. This was what He had tried to tell me beforehand, but I had not paid close enough attention. I came perilously close to experiencing the sinkhole syndrome firsthand! I was also reminded through this experience that no matter where we are in God and no matter how He is using us, He will work to move and stretch us to a new level of abiding in Him. For me it was a long, hard stretch!

The place of abiding

The Apostle John, who had such an understanding of Jesus' heart and seemed to hold a special place in His affections, admonished in one of his later letters,

> *"And now, little children, abide in Him, that when He appears, we may have confidence and not be ashamed before Him at His coming."*   (1 John 2:28)

When God establishes us next to His river, we find what I call "the place of abiding". The place of abiding is the place of unparalleled closeness with God. It is another realm beyond that of the physical realm. It is a place beyond what we can see, hear, feel, taste or touch. It's the place "in Christ". The book of Ephesians more than any other book in the New Testament, explains what it means to be in Christ. We find in this book the inheritance that can be ours in experience as we abide *in Him*. It is a place where we are blessed with every spiritual blessing, where we know we are chosen and adopted, recipients of His grace, redeemed and forgiven, given understanding of His will, sealed with the Holy Spirit, filled with His resurrection power, seated with Jesus in the heavenly places, near to God, and able to come before Him with boldness and confidence. These are just a few of the things we find in the first four chapters of Ephesians that describe the place of abiding *in Him*!

Many of us do not know this place of abiding is available. Or we believe that it is available to everyone else, but for various reasons we feel it is not available to us! For many of us, the thought of being secure, confident, stable and fruitful in our walk with God is just a far off hope. Too often, it seems as though what God has promised is never going to materialize. Repeated failure to grasp a hold of it just reinforces our sense of despair and hopelessness. Sometimes God's people give up and resign themselves to a theology that relegates the place of abiding in Him to eternity. Most of us are familiar with songs like "I'll Fly Away" but are not, perhaps, aware of how unscriptural they are. Of course we have something to look forward to! We will be coming to know Him for eternity! But eternity is only the icing on the cake. The Lord intends for us to begin to receive and experience His riches and His inheritance *now*, in this life. It's all part of abiding *in Him*.

Abiding does not happen automatically

I believe we get it all muddled and tend to think that if He lives in us, it means we are living in Him. These are two different things! The message of the fourth and fifth chapters of Ephesians is, "*If* you have received Him and He lives in you, *then walk in Him*." The book of Ephesians reveals a progression: sit, walk and stand. Because we are seated with Him now legally in the heavenly places, we can walk in that place of abiding and live "in Him". Micah 5 speaks in a beautifully poetic way of the coming Messiah,

> "And He shall stand and feed His flock
> In the strength of the LORD,
> In the majesty of the name of the LORD His God;
> **And they shall abide.**"   (Micah 5:4)

The Hebrew word translated "abide" is in a verb form that has the connotation of *sitting* or remaining. Even the prophetic words of the Old Testament revealed God's plan for us to be seated with Him in the heavenly places as we abide *in Him*! As we abide in that place, we are then able to stand against every enemy onslaught, against every setback and every obstacle. Psalm 91:1 says,

> "He who dwells in the secret place of the Most High
> **Shall abide** under the shadow of the Almighty."

The psalm carries on to describe how it is a place of security and protection from the wiles and strategies of the enemy against us.

The Word says that *in Him* we live and move and have our being, but this is not automatic! It is part of our legal inheritance as sons and joint heirs with Christ. It is part of God's plan and purpose for us. However, it is conditional on our response to Him. So often, we blame God or blame the circumstances for our inability to walk in that kind of connection with Him. Yet the problem is with *us*, not with Him.

▶ *It is something that becomes our experience **as we work out our salvation and allow Him to work His salvation into us!***

It's like having a heavenly bank account. His inheritance has been legally set to our account, but it does not become ours in experience until we write checks against it by faith. We must trust that what He has promised is actually there and then begin to draw upon that account.

For example, when I first began to minister in deliverance, I only knew what the Bible said about having authority over all the power of the enemy. When the Holy Spirit first prompted me to command a spirit to leave someone, I had to trust that His resources were in my heavenly bank account. I had to trust that I had the authority *in Him* to actually deal with a demonic entity. I had to draw upon that account, in essence write a check against it, by stepping out in faith and commanding the spirit to go. Do you know what I found? The resources were in my account!

Fighting to abide

This place of abiding is a place we must fight for. Many of us would rather not have to fight for anything. I have to raise my hand and say, "That's me!" I am a pacifist by nature. I do not like conflict; I do not relish exerting myself; nor do I enjoy being put into a position where I am forced to fight. Every time I find myself in a situation where I have to fight for something, I inwardly groan and plead with the Lord, "Oh, not again! Can't You let it be easy for once?" I suspect I am not alone in my feelings! So we resign ourselves to having to fight for it, but how do we do that?

There are segments of the Body of Christ who seem to envision every spiritual fight as yelling at the devil. In contrast, an older minister shared in a conference I attended a number of years ago that spiritual warfare is 90% focusing on God and only 10% focusing on the devil. At the time, I weighed the statement, not sure if I was in agreement with it or not. However, my experiences over the last decade have brought me to the same conclusion. While I understand the need for spiritual warfare, recognizing that demonic strongholds exist in individual's lives, in cities and regions, and over nations, I firmly believe there is a balance we each need to find. The devil would love us to put our eyes on him. He just loves all that attention! He knows that as long as our focus is on him we are defeated! No, I've learned that the *real* battle is not to conquer the devil, but to surrender to God. We must fight for the place of abiding by surrendering. We always quote the last part of James 4:7 – *"resist the devil and he will flee"*. However, the first part is even more important because it explains what is required for the devil to flee when we resist him. First we must be submitted to God!

We must also fight for the place of abiding by taking every thought captive to the obedience of Christ (2 Corinthians 10:5). The battleground resides in a very small place – the space between our ears! It is primarily in our mind. This is why the Apostle Paul said we are transformed by the renewing of our minds (Romans 12:2). The word translated "repentance" in the New Testament, the Greek word *metanoia*, literally means a change of mind or a change in thinking. When God is able to renew our thinking and align it with His, then real transformation is able to happen in our lives. When we take every thought captive and put it under the Lordship of Christ, we fight our way into the place of abiding!

Finally, we battle for the place of abiding by making right choices. Joshua exhorted the people, *"choose for yourselves this day whom you will serve"* (Joshua 24:15). He told them they could serve any of the gods of the land or they could choose to serve the Lord. He concluded with a declaration of who *he* was going to serve, *"As for me and my house, we will serve the LORD"*! Today, the choice still remains a personal one. Each one of us individually has to make the choice about who we are going to serve. Further, it is an *active* and a *continuing* choice. Just because we have invited Jesus into our life does not mean that the choice to continue to serve Him is automatically made. A conscious choice has to be made every moment of every day! The Lord once asked me, "Do you know *why* My mercies are new every morning?" Recognizing that He was going to show me something new, I said "no" and did not try to guess as I sometimes do. He went on, "It's because you *need* them new every morning!" So we do! Every day we continually face choices that affect us spiritually and we need His mercy and His grace to be able to stand and make right choices. Moses told the Israelites that they also faced the choice of life or death and blessing or cursing:

> *"I call heaven and earth as witnesses today against you, that I have set before you life and death, blessing and cursing; therefore choose life, that both you and your descendants may live."*
> (Deuteronomy 30:19)

We each face these same choices today. When I choose to yield to fear or frustration or bitterness or worldly thinking or lust or any of the thousand things I can serve rather than God, I have chosen death and cursing over life and blessing. Second Peter 2:19 tells us that a man is a slave to whatever has mastered him. We become slaves to whomever we yield our members (Romans 6:19). In the end, most of our choices still boil down to who we are choosing to serve. Will we be slaves to sin or bondservants of Christ?

A circle around God's heart

Not too long ago, Dave and I took three days out of our busy schedules and hid away in a friend's house near the coast to pray and seek the Lord. During that time, the Lord began to speak to me about a call He is sounding to each of us to come in closer, draw in tighter, and come into unity *with Him*. He spoke quietly, asking me to draw a circle and step into it. Then He whispered to me, "This is a circle around My heart." He told me to pray that His grace would keep me there and that His Spirit would constrain me from stepping out of that place.

I then had a mental picture of a baby in the womb, and realized that the circle around God's heart represented a spiritual womb in which we as His children could experience the security, protection, nurture and growth that an unborn baby experiences in the womb. His life, His mercy, His grace, His love, and His power flow through an invisible lifeline or umbilical cord that connects us to Him when we are in that place. It is a place of total dependence on Him, in the same way an unborn child is totally dependent upon its mother for its life and well-being. I also saw that the process is exactly the opposite of the birthing process in the world. Rather than being born *out* of the womb, we are "born again" *into* this womb, into the circle around His heart, the place of abiding *in Him*. In this place we can laugh at the devil (Psalm 37:12–13), because we are protected, secure and are drawing upon His authority, power, wisdom and grace.

Jesus tied this place of abiding in Him to real freedom in John 8:

> *"Then Jesus said to those Jews who believed Him, 'If you abide in My word, you are My disciples indeed. And you shall know the truth, and the truth shall make you free.'"* (John 8:31–32)

If we abide in His Word *then* we experientially come to know the Truth who is a Person. It is through Him that we find the freedom for which we have sought. He also tied the place of abiding to fruitfulness in John 15:

> *"Abide in Me, and I in you. As the branch cannot bear fruit of itself, unless it abides in the vine, neither can you, unless you abide in Me. I am the vine, you are the branches. He who abides in Me, and I in him, bears much fruit; for without Me you can do nothing."*   (John 15:4–5)

The Greek word for *abide* used here means "to continue in, remain, live in, do not depart from". Jesus says that if we will live *in Him*, if we will remain in that circle around His heart and not depart from that place, we will become those fruit trees who bear much fruit. It is a place that I am personally committed to living in and living out of in increasing measure. How about you?

Prayer

Father, I want to discover and live in that place of abiding in You. I want to step into the circle around Your heart and never step out of it! I want to be that intimate and one with You, dependent upon You as my source for everything pertaining to life and godliness. I want to know and experience for myself the security, the stability and empowerment that You have for me in Christ. I want to know and experience for myself the wealth of the inheritance You have for me as a son and joint heir with Jesus Christ. I want to be fed and watered by the river of God. Father, please forgive me for any way that I have lost touch with the river of Your presence through apathy or carelessness. Help me to connect with You once again, that the sinkhole syndrome might be a thing of the past in my life. Lord, I invite You to come fill the empty places and the void in me with more of You. May Your kingdom come in this earth, in this clay vessel, in a more complete way. Let me be established beside Your river that my walk might be fruitful, prosperous and glorifying to You in every way. Amen.

Chapter 6

Not My Will but Yours

As a new Christian a number of years ago, I found myself in a peculiar situation. I was conversing with a relative who was tentatively exploring Christianity. Feeling quite the expert, as immature Christians often do, I was dying to share some things with her that I thought would be helpful. However, as soon as I went to open my mouth the Holy Spirit gave me a kick and I heard quite clearly in my spirit, "Don't say it!" I shook my head a bit as though to clear it and thought to myself, "Where did that come from?" Then I proceeded to share it anyway! Something in me was determined to plow on, regardless of the consequences. I had a vague sense that the Lord was shushing me, but I did not want to stop and investigate because I really *wanted* to say it! At that moment, I chose my will over His. In the end, there was some trouble over what was said, and I had several opportunities to deeply regret my impulsive decision to ignore the Lord's prompting!

▶ *I've discovered the hard way that this choice, **our will or His,** is critical if we want to move from nominal Christianity to apprehending the inheritance He provided for us at Calvary.*

We face choices every day of our lives. Some are big. Some seem small. But *all* are a doorway! They are either a doorway for the kingdom of God to come more fully in our lives, or a doorway through which death slips in and works in us. The New Testament reveals that the fruit or consequence of sin is death (Romans 6:23; James 1:15). Fundamentally, we reap what we sow. If we opt for independence from God, choosing to yield to our self-will and go our own way, spiritual death will begin to work in our lives through that decision no matter how small it might seem. Some of us choose our own way many times on a daily basis, week after week, month after month, sometimes even year after year. Then we wonder why we have so many problems and are not experiencing victory in our walk with the Lord!

The enemy's subtle trap

Satan once occupied the place of spiritual priesthood similar to the one we now occupy (see Ezekiel 28:11–19). The New Testament describes those who carry the name of Jesus as a *"holy priesthood"*, a *"royal priesthood"*, and *"kings and priests"* before God (1 Peter 2:5, 9; Revelation 1:6; 5:10). We are, as His priests, called to worship Him and offer up spiritual sacrifices (1 Peter 2:5; Hebrews 13:15). The Ezekiel 28 passage indicates that Lucifer, now called Satan, may have held a position similar to that of a worship leader in heaven (Ezekiel 28:13–15). Lucifer means "light-bearer". He was once an archangel who was cast out of heaven when he stood against God in pride and self-will (Isaiah 14:12–15). Now our enemy and the enemy of God, he wants to see us disqualified from the place of spiritual priesthood in the same way he was disqualified. How does he do this? He accomplishes this feat by tempting and influencing us to yield to pride and self-will! He will try his best to ensnare us with these things to keep us from stepping into the place of spiritual authority reserved for God's royal priesthood.

The example of Jesus

Jesus, by contrast, came in the opposite spirit to Lucifer. He came with a humble heart and a desire to yield to the Father's will rather than His own. His desire to submit to the Father's will was tested in a major way just before He was arrested and sent to the cross. It happened in the Garden of Gethsemane. There in this garden, He agonized in prayer over the decision to submit to the Father's will, to the point of shedding drops of blood. Jesus did not approach the cross lightly. Knowing what the cost would be to Himself, He was distressed and anguished by the decision He faced. But in the end He submitted His will to the Father's, saying, *"nevertheless not My will, but Yours, be done"* (Luke 22:42).

My husband, Dave, has shared with many how the Lord showed him one day that the victory was not really won at Calvary. It was won before that, in Gethsemane when Jesus submitted Himself unconditionally to His Father's will. It was then sealed and finished at Calvary. Our own making of the choice to submit to the Father's will in the everyday situations we face, is where our own victory is won. Christian lives that glorify God begin with this choice, "not my will but Yours, Lord." Further, it is fundamental to experiencing and walking in the inheritance He has for us!

Being set free from the law of sin and death

There is a process, however, that has to take place in our lives before we are able to regularly choose His will over our own. I used to beat myself up regularly because I stumbled at every turn and seemed to always make wrong choices. I hated myself because I could never seem to get it right! We find in Romans 7 that the Apostle Paul struggled with the same thing. He said that he did not do the things he *wanted* to do, and the things he did *not* want to do he did anyway! He cried out, *"O wretched man that I am! Who will deliver me from this body of death?"* (Romans 7:24). He then goes on to answer this question in the last verses of this chapter, and in the first verses of Romans 8. He praises God for Jesus Christ and His finished work that allows the law of the Spirit of life to set him free from that law of sin and death working in him. This spiritual law supercedes the law of sin and death in much the same way that the physical law of aerodynamics supercedes the law of gravity. When a plane takes off, the higher law of aerodynamics overshadows and supercedes the law of gravity. Similarly, the law of the Spirit of life in Christ Jesus enables us, when we step into the realm of the kingdom of God, to defy the law of sin and death that would work in us!

▶ *The more we are filled with Him, the more effectively we can defy the law of sin and death.*

John the Baptist said, *"I must decrease that He might increase"* (John 3:30). What is needed is less of us and more of Him! The more there is of Him in us, the easier we will find it to submit our wills to His. The more we submit our wills to His, the more He is able to fill us with His life and power!

A painful learning experience

When our children were small, we moved from southern Nevada to New Mexico. We transitioned from several years of apartment living into a rental house with a big yard. Dave and I had found it necessary to give away our dogs when we first moved into an apartment, and I missed them very much. I was very eager for the opportunity to have a dog again. But there was a big problem – our landlords did not want any pets! I was all right with their decision until two Siberian Huskies in the community had puppies. Every week we would drive by the cutest puppies in the world and my heart would melt every time I saw them!

After a time, all the puppies were sold except one. I began to scheme, something I am very good at when I don't have my carnal nature under control. I convinced myself that God *wanted* me to have this puppy. After all, it looked like He had saved this puppy just for me! Further, didn't He say in the book of Proverbs that He wants to give us the desires of our hearts? Our landlords did not want the puppy in their rental house, Dave didn't particularly want the puppy, but *I* wanted the puppy and I intended to keep plugging away until something happened! I never asked the Lord about the dog because I was afraid he might say "no". I was determined to get what I wanted, even if it meant acting independently of God or deluding myself that this was His idea.

I finally won over Dave and the landlords, and the exciting day arrived when our lovely puppy was to be brought home. By this time, the Husky pup was five months old and fairly big. We named him Meshach, a nice biblical name that we hoped would influence his nature and character. It didn't work. From the first day, Meshach was one gigantic headache after another! He chewed a big hole in the seat of Dave's recliner, the only nice piece of furniture we owned. Then he went on to destroy the couch. When he started on the baseboards, doors and carpets of our rental house, we began to panic! We got permission from the landlords to put him outside, as long as we kept him on the patio and off the newly planted lawn (which entailed the time and expense of building a fence).

There was a further problem. Meshach had continual diarrhea from the first day we brought him home. Every day I would come home from work in the winter cold and sleet to find diarrhea everywhere that had to be cleaned up! We thought at first it had to do with the transition from mother's milk to Puppy Chow. However, when there was no change after 3–4 weeks, we took him to the vet. There, we were given the astounding news that Meshach was born with a non-functioning pancreas! The only hope, according to the vet, was a synthetic hormone that had only a 50% success rate and would cost $75 a month. In 1983, this figure represented our food budget for the month! We took Meshach home from the vet's office and continued to clean up diarrhea every day from the patio as we tried to figure out our next step. We prayed for him. We had other people pray for him. We gnashed our teeth, bit our fingernails and finally decided we just could not afford the medication that might or might not work.

Meanwhile, another problem surfaced – as if there weren't enough already! Every time the dog saw poor Lauren, who was only 3 years old, he would take a flying leap, knock her over and start biting her ears! The house was continually punctuated with her screams and we really feared that he was traumatizing her.

The final straw came after we had owned Meshach about eight or nine weeks. The neighbor behind us mentioned one day that Meshach barked – a lot. Upon questioning, it came to light that Meshach barked *all* day, *every* day while we were away at work. The neighbors had simply been too nice to complain. That was it! Meshach was found another home and I learned my lesson about plowing ahead independently of God without asking Him about His will in a particular matter. I learned from this experience that the consequences of getting what I want can be disastrous and very painful!

It's the heart attitude that counts!

For a long time in my Christian walk, I could only hear the "no's" from God. I knew pretty clearly when He was giving me a check or letting me know that something was *not* His will, though my paying attention to it was another matter. The "yes's" however were much harder to discern. It took a number of years of walking with the Lord before I could begin to be sure when the Lord was prompting me with a directive or a direction. It was especially confusing if what He was telling me coincided with my own desires! Then it was very hard indeed and I often had to appeal to an objective third party, asking them to pray about it with me. For many years, I agonized over making a mistake and getting it wrong. Getting it wrong in the early years of my walk with God had caused such huge problems! Also, through the ensuing years He had truly captivated my heart, and I did not want to grieve or dishonor Him in any way by taking a wrong step. Further, I was still very much a perfectionist and fearful of failure. I found, however, with the Lord's continual reassurance that it was not perfection He wanted. It was my heart! I learned that if my heart was to obey and choose His will, He would cover any mistakes I made. Just recently, I lay in bed one night crying out to Him in distress and agony of heart, telling Him, "Lord, I want to do Your will but I don't know what Your will is in this matter." Silently, I was calling out to Him, "Help!" Within a day, I began to see His will clearly. He brought much grace into the situation and it was able to be resolved without much difficulty. It's the honesty and sincerity of our hearts which cause Him to respond, not our flawlessness or perfection. Understanding this can free us from the paralysis that comes from thinking we always have to get it right. It can liberate us to respond to the Lord at the risk of making a mistake.

Maturity means a willingness to give up our own way

The place we run into trouble is the one in which we are determined to get what we want and no one, not even God, is going to stop us. I sometimes see little children in the grocery stores throwing temper tantrums to manipulate their mothers into giving them what they want. We learn at a young age, don't we? I'm not sure that all the adults filling our pews or church chairs have grown past this. I've seen a number of tantrums in my years in the ministry! They are, of course, more subtle and polished than what is evident in the grocery store, but they are still a vivid demonstration of self-will in action. When people go off in a huff, withdraw in resentment or release their tongue in spiteful anger, it is just the adult version of a temper tantrum. Self is screaming, "I want my way!" Some people don't throw tantrums. They just quietly go about their business, making sure they get what they want in hopes that the Lord will not notice what they are doing if they don't draw attention to themselves. Young people will often approach the "my will versus God's will" choices this way. I cannot recall how many Christian girls I have seen falter and fall away from the Lord because they were determined to date a particular boy no matter what His heart and mind on the matter might be. They set their will and that was that. It was all done very quietly, but it was just as deadly to their spiritual well being.

Putting things on God's altar

One thing I have learned is that we often don't get what we really want until we are willing to put things on the altar and truly submit our wills to His. The Lord called Abraham to put His promise (Isaac) on the altar and be willing to allow the son of promise to die (Genesis 22). Of course, he was stopped after he had demonstrated his willingness to be obedient and we know that Isaac did not die. But the Lord sometimes allows the things *we* are putting *our* hope in to die. The Apostle Paul told the Roman church that obedience leads to righteousness (Romans 6:16). Abraham's obedience and choice to believe God, no matter what, was counted to him as righteousness (Galatians 3:2). Righteousness is worked into our lives as we make the choice to put our desires, our hopes, our vision and everything the Lord has given us on the altar in obedience and simple trust in Him. We will look at this concept more in depth in chapter 9.

When Dave and I lived near Las Vegas, Nevada, we became desperate at one point to get out of the desert and back to the mountains. Any mountains would do! It became an obsession. We told the Lord over and over how much we wanted it, needed it, *had* to get back to the mountains for our happiness and sanity. Every avenue we tried, however, fell apart. Everything that looked promising would finally falter and come to nothing. We grew more and more discouraged. Some time later, we were due to meet Dave's family in Colorado for a week of camping and hiking on the Conejos River. One bright afternoon, while the rest of the family were watching our children, Dave and I hiked up the trail to a massive boulder that must have been thirty feet high. We managed to scramble to the top, where we sat holding hands as we prayed and submitted our hearts and lives to the Lord in a fresh way. We both sensed that God wanted us to lay our desire to live in the mountains again on the altar and choose His will, whatever it might be. So we sat there and prayed and we told the Lord that if He wanted us to stay in the desert for the rest of our lives we would gladly do it. Further, we *meant* it! We had finally come to a place where it was His will that mattered to us more than anything else. A week later, a job and a place to live sovereignly opened up for us in the mountains of northern New Mexico.

Choices, choices, and more choices

There are so many areas of choice we face in our lives. It's not just about pets, jobs, geographical moves, or what we say or don't say. The willingness to choose His will instead of our own impacts *every* area of our lives. Are we willing to stretch out of our comfort zones to choose the narrow path of life and blessing? Are we willing to accept by faith that what He says is true, even when everything we see seems to shout that it is not? Are we willing to be thankful when we would love to wallow in self-pity? Are we willing to allow Him to do things His way and not our way? Are we willing to lay down our lives for others in honor, preferring them and serving them? Are we willing to let go of things we think we have a right to hold onto, like the right to whine or hold a grudge? These are the "little" choices we face on a daily basis that make us or break us. They make us big people or little people. His will or our own? The choice is ours.

▶ *It is a choice that often determines how much of His inheritance we are able to firmly possess in our lives!*

His will is always best

It has taken many mistakes through the years for me to finally come to the realization that His way is truly the best way. Many times it does not look that way at the outset, however! The time that stands out the clearest in my mind is when He called us to go to Bible College in Texas. I did not want to go! We had moved around a lot in the early years of our marriage and we were finally in a place that I liked and wanted to stay. We had just bought our first house and had been in it only a year. We had two young children to look after, and I couldn't fathom how we could go back to school and still support our young, growing family. The Bible College in question was in a big city in another state where we had no friends or family. In contrast, we lived very close to Dave's family in New Mexico. We were also part of a lovely church that had an incredible revelation of worship. I looked forward to that worship time with the Lord every week because it was so awesome. Why would anyone want to give so much up and go somewhere else? I certainly did not! Dave, however, was certain he had heard clearly from the Lord and prayed for me until the Lord changed my heart. Our house sold in less than a week and within a few months we were off to Dallas with our two kids, two Golden Retrievers and U-Haul full of furniture. All bridges were burned behind us! I was still a little panicky about it, though. What if we got there and it was awful? We had given up so much that was dear to follow the leading of the Lord. Our first Sunday there finally arrived and we tenta-tively slipped into the service. About half way through it, as I was basking in the presence of the Lord and reveling in the depth of worship, the Lord nudged me. "What do you think?" He asked. "Oh, it is wonderful!" I responded. "I have never been in a worship service like this before!" At that point, He reminded me how resistant I had been and with subtle humor continued, "See, Dee, I really do have better things for you than you would choose for yourself!"

If we will only choose His will over our own, we can each discover the truth of this statement for ourselves. He is such a good God, so full of mercy and grace. It is there for us to see, to unfold, to embrace and to experience – if we will but walk with Him *His* way!

Prayer

Lord, I offer to You all the times I have chosen to go my own way and sought what I wanted over what You wanted. I lay those choices at Your feet and ask You to forgive me and cleanse me of all unrighteousness. I pray that You will help me and enable me by the power of Your Spirit to choose Your will over my own. Please help me to believe You and be obedient to You, that Your righteousness might be worked into my life. Help me to be more aware of the "little" choices I face on a daily basis which make or break me. I pray You will give me eyes to see each choice as a doorway to life or death. Help me to embrace the Spirit of Life in Christ Jesus that the law of sin and death might be overcome in my life. Change my heart, O God. I want to be willing to put everything You have promised and everything You have given on the altar. I want only You and Your will to reign supreme in my life. Amen.

Chapter 7

Learning to Walk in His Authority

The first glimpse I received of personally walking in God's authority was in Mexico in 1988. Dave and I were members of a team of students sent to the state of Guerrero to learn firsthand about the mission field. We also hoped to be a blessing to the people there as we ministered in different villages. Near the beginning of our stay we walked from house to house, inviting people to a service at the local evangelical church. At one house, a couple who were obviously worried and distressed, asked us if we would pray for their sick baby. The poor child was burning with fever and clearly desperately ill. We all laid hands on the baby and prayed fervently for the Lord to touch him. I wish I could say that we were instantly aware of the power of God coursing through us to bring life and health to his little body, but I cannot! We just prayed in faith and went on to the next house. About half way through the service, several hours later, a distraught man rushed in, interrupting the worship. I didn't recognize him at first. He was speaking loudly and rapidly in Spanish, gesturing wildly, and acting like a madman. I couldn't make out what was going on. Suddenly, all the men around him who were listening began to grin broadly, then laugh and give thanks the God. The whole place then began to rejoice. It was the father of the sick baby coming to tell the church that the Lord had completely healed his son! A miracle took place before the couple's eyes as we had moved on to the next house.

Learning to walk in God's authority is imperative if we are to apprehend and live in His kingdom. Jesus said, *"the kingdom of heaven suffers violence, and the violent take it by force"* (Matthew 11:12). His kingdom must be pursued, grabbed hold of and possessed in an active, forceful way. To inherit the kingdom, we must get out of our defensive posture and go on the offensive!

People who enjoy American football know how important it is to have a good offensive line. I graduated from the University of Georgia, a place renowned for football. Everything seemed to revolve around football in Athens, Georgia in the 1970s! When there was a home game, all the stores would broadcast the game over an intercom system so that shoppers could keep up with the score play by play. I learned a lot about football there. I learned that a good defense will not win the game. It takes an aggressive offense, as well as solid defense, to see victory. Sadly, many Christians have not learned this. They live their lives on the defensive, trying to hold off the kingdom of darkness from impinging on their lives. That is not enough. It is merely playing defensive football. You might keep your opponent from scoring, but you never score either! To see victory in this Christian walk, we must go on the offensive, aggressively pursuing the kingdom of God! This means we need to understand the authority He has delegated to us, His Body.

Genesis – origins of our authority

The book of Genesis, which literally means "beginning", is considered the seedbed of the entire Bible. Every biblical truth can be found in seed form in the book of Genesis. If we study it closely, we will discover that God's original plan for mankind is imbedded in the Genesis creation account. This account reveals what He intended for us from the beginning, before His purposes for mankind were derailed by man's fall into sin. For this reason, it is important to look at what the book of Genesis reveals about the authority God gave mankind. It shows us the place of authority that Jesus came to restore!

In Genesis 1, we see that man was made in the image and likeness of God. The likeness was spiritual, intellectual, emotional and moral. Most scholars agree that it was also a likeness in authority, since 'adam (the Hebrew word for human beings or mankind) was given authority over the earth and living things. In a very real sense, God's purpose for mankind from the beginning was for man to be *like* Him – to share His heart, mind, will and purposes, and to have His character and His nature.

When God breathed His breath of life into the dust of the ground to create *'adam* (Genesis 2:7), He was imparting *Himself* into mankind. God is our source. He is the spiritual substance out of which mankind was initially formed. We were taken out of God, a family to be united with Him and sustained by Him for eternity. This was His plan from before the creation of the world!

At creation, both man and woman were given joint dominion over the earth by God (Genesis 1:27–28). They were told to *"subdue"* the earth. The Hebrew tense used means "to bring into subjection, to make subservient, to dominate or tread down". The imperative mood used means that it was issued as an order or a command. It was not merely a privilege or a suggestion! Then, in the next sentence, mankind was told to *"have dominion"* over *"every living thing"* on the earth. A different Hebrew word was used, but it similarly describes ruling, dominating, treading down, subjugating and having dominion over. Again, it was issued in the form of an order or a command. This is what God intended when He made man. He purposed for us to share in His authority over the rest of creation! What happened then? Where did the divine plan get off track?

Adam and Eve had authority because they were under God's authority, in union with and connected to Him. They had intrinsic authority as those *like* Him and in His image. They had delegated authority as His representatives on the earth. All that changed, however, when they chose to walk out from under His authority and come under Satan's authority through their self-will and disobedience! This is when Satan gained the right to become *"the god of this world"* (2 Corinthians 4:4, KJV). It is also when the image of God in mankind shattered and became distorted, like the pieces of a broken mirror heaped upon the floor. From the fall onward, mankind was then born in Adam's fallen image (Genesis 5:3), under Satan's authority, and into his domain. That is the state we all found ourselves in until we were translated by the blood of Jesus Christ from the kingdom of darkness into the kingdom of God (Colossians 1:13).

The provision our Creator made at Calvary through the death of His Son was to make a way for us back to His original intent and purpose.

▶ *Jesus made a way for us back to Plan A!*

Through Him, we can be re-connected with the Father, once again in unity with Him and sustained by Him. Upon death of our physical bodies, we will be assimilated back into God for eternity, fulfilling His original plan. Through Jesus, our intrinsic authority is restored as we become conformed to His image once again (Romans 8:29). Through Him, our delegated authority is also recovered as we begin to understand the depth and magnitude of the Good News and appropriate it for ourselves. Through His blood we are set free to stand once again as children of God, His representatives on the earth, with His blessing and authority to take dominion over creation! This authority is over both natural things (Genesis 1:27–28; Psalm 8) and spiritual things (Psalm 149; Luke 10:19; 1 Corinthians 6:3).

In the Old Testament, this authority came only with a special anointing given to special men by God to accomplish a specific task. Joshua could command the sun to stand still and it obeyed (Joshua 10:12–13), because he had a special anointing from God to lead the people of Israel in possessing the land of promise. Elijah had command over the rain (1 Kings 17:1; James 5:17) and Elisha could raise the child of the Shunamite woman from the dead (2 Kings 4:32–37) because they were anointed by the Spirit of God as His representatives on the earth at that time. However, in this New Testament dispensation of grace, *all* those who have received Christ and embraced His Holy Spirit can have this anointing! The Holy Spirit doesn't just rest on a few special handpicked people. He now can indwell and empower every believer! We can *all* be God's representatives or ambassadors on the earth (2 Corinthians 5:20). This is why Jesus, who had authority over the elements, over sickness and disease, over death and the demonic, could tell each one of His disciples:

> *"Most assuredly, I say to you, he who believes in Me, the works that I do he will do also; **and greater works than these he will do**, because I go to My Father."*　　　　(John 14:12)

As His disciples, each one of us has the potential to do greater things than Jesus did on the earth. That is not my opinion; it is what Jesus Himself said. Let's take the limitations off our thinking and begin to think like Jesus!

Jesus' delegation of authority to His Body

Daniel prophesied of the coming Messiah,

> *"Then to Him was given dominion, glory and a kingdom . . .*
> *His dominion is an everlasting dominion,*
> *Which shall not pass away,*
> *And His kingdom the one*
> *Which shall not be destroyed."*   (Daniel 7:14)

The Chaldee word translated *dominion* means "to govern, to prevail or to dominate". Through His dominion and eternal government, Jesus' ambassadors have the opportunity to once again stand in a place of authority in this earth. Jesus shared in John 5:26–30 that His authority is derived from the Father's. Because He and the Father are one, and He does not act independently of the Father, He has the same authority. It works the same way with us. Our authority in the earth is now derived from that of Jesus. If we become one with Him, and do not act independently of Him, we have the same authority!

Daniel 7:22 further describes the vision Daniel had of the future. He speaks prophetically about the devil *"making war against the saints"* and notes that he was prevailing against them *until* Jesus (called the Ancient of Days) came. A judgement was then made and *"the time came for the saints to possess the kingdom"*. Saints, that judgement was made at Calvary! The time *has* come for the saints to possess God's kingdom! Jesus' message during His three years of ministry on the earth was that the kingdom of heaven is "at hand". *That means here and now.* He said to pray that His kingdom would come on the earth. How is that going to happen? It will only happen as we unite ourselves with Him and stand in His authority. This uniting and standing must move beyond something we understand and acknowledge intellectually, however, to something that is *real* in us and permeates every part of our lives at the most basic level! It must move beyond wishful thinking to life-impacting reality.

The Bible is, more than anything else, a legal document. It shows us what our inheritance is – what legally belongs to us as

God's children and co-heirs with Christ. The second chapter of Ephesians gives us some specifics about this inheritance. Ephesians 2:5–6 reveals that, *legally*, those who are born again are in union with the risen Lord in three ways:

- in His victory over sin and death,
- in His resurrection, and
- in His rule at the Father's right hand.

In the previous chapter of Ephesians, this place was described as *"far above all principality and power and might and dominion, and every name that is named, not only in this age but also in that which is to come"* (Ephesians 1:21). This means that *legally* we occupy a place of authority over every demonic principality and power and every named thing. It has nothing to do with us, but everything to do with Him! It is because *His* is the name above all names. It is because we as His Body are lifted up with Him. Because all things are under His feet, they are under our feet as well (Ephesians 1:21–22). Jesus said, *"All authority has been given to Me in heaven and on earth"* (Matthew 28:18). He then delegated this authority to us as His Body!

We see a demonstration of this delegated authority in the sending out of the twelve disciples. Matthew 10, Mark 6 and Luke 9 are all parallel accounts that record this event, though each somewhat differently as is always the case with eyewitness accounts. According to Matthew, He called them to Himself, then *"gave them power over unclean spirits, to cast them out, and to heal all kinds of sickness and all kinds of disease"* (Matthew 10:1). *"All"* means all! *Every* sickness and *every* disease was subject to their authority. He told them, *"As you go, preach ... heal the sick, cleanse the lepers, raise the dead, cast out demons. Freely you have received, freely give"* (Matthew 10:7–8). Later, He sent out the seventy (or seventy-two as some of the Greek manuscripts read) with the same authority and the same commission. They returned, excited that they had authority over demons in His name. Some would try to limit this authority to the early Church. But two thousand years of history denies this assertion. Believers throughout history, in all corners of the globe, have operated in this same authority!

Needed: simple faith, submission and backbone!

Legally, His authority is part of our inheritance as saints of God. What we live out of is another matter! So often, we live far below our privileges. We have been given the unfathomable riches of Christ (Ephesians 3:8), the riches of His goodness (Romans 2:4), the riches of His glory (Ephesians 3:16; Romans 9:23), and the riches of His grace (Ephesians 1:7; 2:7). However, despite all this spiritual wealth, we often live below the poverty level. We act like beggars, pleading with God for a handout! Jesus said at the cross, *"It is finished!"* (John 19:30). His work is done. The inheritance has been bought and paid for, a salvation given freely by God to those who will receive it. A look at the original Greek language reveals to us that this salvation encompasses healing, deliverance, and wholeness, as well as rescue from hell. But we have to *"work out"* our salvation (Philippians 2:12). The Greek quite literally means "do what it takes to make it happen"! It's up to us to appropriate what Jesus purchased for us. It's up to us to pursue His kingdom. It's up to us to grab hold of what's been stolen by the enemy in our lives and take it back.

We legally have the authority. What we don't always have is the *belief* that we have it! I have pondered long and hard over why we see so many miracles and healings in third world countries and so little in the prosperous west. I believe it has to do with "simple faith". Those who lead simple, uncomplicated lives often seem to have a very simple, uncomplicated faith. The Word says it, they believe it, and that is the end of it as far as they are concerned. Those of us in the western Church, however, often find our minds suddenly filled with theological arguments, intellectual debates and every conceivable rationale the minute we begin to pray for someone. Our lives are very complicated and we seem to extend that complication to our faith. Yet what did the Apostle Paul write to the Corinthian church about this very thing? He wrote,

> *"But I fear, lest somehow, as the serpent deceived Eve by his craftiness, so your minds may be corrupted from the simplicity that is in Christ."*   (2 Corinthians 11:3)

There is a simplicity in the message of the gospel that we can easily miss. Wrapping ourselves up in intellectualism, rationalism and theological arguments can hinder us from understanding what it means to walk in His authority.

Another thing that we frequently find missing in our lives is the submission that is key to unlocking this authority!

▶ *Like Adam and Eve, the level of dominion we walk in is directly proportional to our level of submission to God.*

If we remove ourselves from union and intimacy with God in pride and independence, the same spiritual death and loss of authority seen in Adam and Eve's lives will be seen in ours! As mentioned in a previous chapter, it is only as we submit to God that the devil will flee (James 4:17).

Finally, though we legally have His authority, we don't always have the backbone to stand in it! Many times we act like spiritual wimps rather than the spiritual warriors we were ordained to be. Though Jesus called us to intimidate the enemy and cause him to flee, many of us are the ones who are intimidated and running. We are called to be more than conquerors (Romans 8:37). We are called to overcome! Jesus overcame and as we stand in His authority, we are also conquerors. He said,

> *"To him who overcomes I will grant to sit with Me on My throne, as I also overcame and sat down with My Father on His throne."*
> (Revelation 3:21)

He continued later,

> *"He who overcomes shall inherit all things, and I will be his God and he shall be My son."*   (Revelation 21:7)

In the Apostle John's vision, the end-time saints overcame the devil and his kingdom by the blood of the Lamb and the word of their testimony (Revelation 12:11). They were overcomers!

Too often, however, we go to our pastors or other church leaders, wanting them to pray for us, relying on *their* faith and *their* authority, instead of learning to walk in our own. I think that is why so many of us stay leveled by the enemy, walking around depressed and defeated. It is imperative that we each press into the presence of God and get His revelation in our hearts about the authority He purchased for us. It cannot stop there, though! Once we can see it clearly and it is firmly anchored in our hearts, we still must commit to walk in it. It *is* easier to whine and complain, or to give up with our tail tucked between our legs. Yet if we are committed to walking in this authority of His, we will push through the flesh and the fear to take a stand in the power of the Holy Spirit!

Executors of the Father's will

We see one of God's eternal purposes for the Church in Ephesians 3. He says His intent is thus,

> *"that now the manifold wisdom of God might be made known by the church to the principalities and powers in the heavenly places, according to the eternal purpose which He accomplished in Christ Jesus our Lord, in whom we have boldness and access with confidence through faith in Him."* (Ephesians 3:10–12)

We are called to serve notice to the kingdom of darkness! A study of the New Testament reveals that every Christian has these three enemies – the world, the flesh and the devil. Have you ever gotten an eviction notice? An eviction notice means that the person on the receiving end of it has no legal right to dwell in, inhabit or occupy a place anymore. The world, the flesh and the devil are overdue for eviction notices in some of our lives! They've been occupying our bodily temples and influencing our actions for a long time. But it is time to serve them notice! God directs His people to make no covenant with their enemies (Deuteronomy 7:1–2), but many of us have done so without realizing it. It's time to break that friendship and agreement with the world, the flesh and the devil in our lives. It is time to evict them and their influence!

Psalm 149 gives us a beautiful picture of the authority we have over God's enemies as executors of His will who enforce His judgement and His decrees. This psalm describes how praise and His Word are spiritual weapons that bind and bring about His judgement on His enemies. It concludes that *all* saints have this honor or privilege. We all have the privilege or authority to enforce the victory won at Calvary. Colossians 2:15 says,

"Having disarmed principalities and powers, He made a public spectacle of them, triumphing over them in it."

He has taken the keys to death and hell away from Satan and now holds them in His hand (Revelation 1:18). The judgement has been made in the heavenlies. Our part, then, is to bind and loose on earth what has already been bound and loosed in heaven (Matthew 16:19; 18:18–20), and to co-labor with the Lord that His kingdom might become manifest or visible on this earth (Matthew 6:10).

In the 1970s, Jack Hayford wrote a book called *Prayer is Invading the Impossible*. I love this book because it changed my life! Pastor Hayford writes,

> "But He [Jesus] did teach them something about a matter of violence. He was very clear on that one thing. Prayer was a matter of assault, of binding, of warfare, of invasion. On earthside, He taught, things may appear impossible, yet, from the heavenside of things, there is a violence that can explode the impossible. But it needs troops for the invasion . . . His purpose is repossession . . . Each believer is a member of an occupational force which has one principle purpose: to enforce the victory of Calvary. It is in this context that prayer begins to take shape."[1]

In our first pastorate, somebody gave me another book by a man who had been a pilot in the Pacific during World War II. He too spoke about enforcing the victory of Calvary. He shared some parallels between what happened at the end of World War II, and our position as Christians. When the Japanese surrendered, victory was declared by the Allied forces. The war was truly over. On many of the islands scattered throughout the Pacific, however, there remained enemy troops occupying these islands that were not about to come out with their hands up! The war was legally over, but the victory still had to be enforced. Allied troops had to invade these islands to route out the enemy. Because of the victory that had been won, they had the authority to do this. But if they had never gone into those jungles to enforce the victory, the enemy would still be in there occupying those places illegally! This is true of our lives and our communities as well. If we don't enforce Christ's victory at Calvary and stand through our inter-cession in the authority He has delegated to us as His Body, the world, the flesh and the devil will occupy places in our lives that God purposed for Himself.

In God's economy right makes might!

The New Testament makes a clear distinction between authority and power. Authority is right. It is a legal position. Power is might. In the world it is said that "might makes right". In the spiritual world, however, it is right that makes might! Jesus told the disciples in Luke 10:19 that He was giving them authority or right (Greek: *exousia*), over all the power or might (Greek: *dunamis*), of the enemy. *Exousia*, the word used for authority here, is from a root meaning "lawful". It is the legal right to use *dunamis* (power)! An example would be that of a policeman. The policeman has the legal right to use force to administer the law. The whole government of the nation is behind him. This is why he has authority. We may observe that a traffic cop has very little power when you compare his size and weight to that of the automobiles bearing down upon him! But because he has *author-ity*, the drivers of those automobiles normally obey his directives. They know that he represents the government. And if they disobey him, they will have to contend with the government. It is the same in the spiritual realm. We have authority as God's representatives on earth. Even though we may have very little power in terms of human strength or ability, the government of heaven stands behind us as ambassadors with His authority!

Jesus operated in both *exousia* (authority), and *dunamis* (power), according to Luke 4:36. It wasn't one without the other. He then gave His disciples both *exousia* and *dunamis* (Luke 9:1). The English words "dynamite" and "dynamic" both come from the Greek word *dunamis*. Some concordances define it as "inherent power" or "miracle-working power". It is important to note, though, that this power is not natural human strength, ability, or wisdom but the power of the Holy Spirit. The Apostle Paul said,

> *"But we have this treasure in earthen vessels, that the excellence of the power may be of God and not of us."* (2 Corinthians 4:7)

We have this same Holy Spirit and He will empower us with the same *dunamis* power out of which Jesus operated. He told His disciples,

> **"But you shall receive power when the Holy Spirit has come upon you**; *and you shall be witnesses to Me in Jerusalem, and in all Judea and Samaria, and to the end of the earth."*
>
> (Acts 1:8)

There is empowerment that comes into our lives with the Holy Spirit. It is not just power over sin, but it is power to be His witnesses. It is supernatural power. It is divine power. It is effective, active, penetrating, immeasurable and unstoppable! The Apostle Paul explained in 1 Corinthians 4:20 that the kingdom of God is not a matter of talk but of power. The Lord has given us His power to be people who would not just *talk* big, but be people that will *walk* big!

We have been given both His authority and His power to be all He has called us to be, and to accomplish everything He has called us to do. His divine power has given to us *everything* pertaining to life and godliness (2 Peter 1:3). That means that everything we need, we have – legally. Our lives can be a radical demonstration of His life and power to a lost and dying world, if we will, with submitted hearts and lives, learn to walk in His authority!

Prayer

Lord, I want to learn to walk in Your authority. I confess to You that I have been satisfied with less than You have purposed for me. I recognize that Your plan for me from the beginning was to rule and reign with You, but that this plan was derailed by mankind's sin in the Garden of Eden. I embrace and appropriate for myself the blood of Jesus today, that I might be restored to Your original plan. I choose to step into that place as Your representative on this earth. I choose to be an ambassador for Christ today. I open my life to receive and walk in the delegated authority I have been given as a member of Your body. I humbly submit my life to You. I choose to let go of rationalism, intellectualism and my need to figure everything out. I choose to let go of fear or anything else that has hindered me from walking in Your authority. I ask You, Lord, to help me be the spiritual warrior You have called me to be. I desire to be one who would stand firm to enforce the victory won at Calvary and to be an executor of the Father's will. I choose to allow my praise and confession to execute God's written judgement upon the kingdom of darkness. I choose to be a vessel through whom You can work to accomplish Your purposes in the earth. Holy Spirit, I invite You to fill me and keep filling me, that Your *dunamis* power might be resident within me. I truly desire my life to stand as a testimony of Your abundant life and supernatural power at work within me. Amen.

Note

1. Jack Hayford, *Prayer is Invading the Impossible* (Logos International, Plainfield, NJ, 1977), pp. 12, 15, 18.

Chapter 8

The Insidious Disease

The accounts recorded in Mark 6 reveal some very interesting things about Jesus and the dynamics of the spiritual world. The power of unbelief is exposed through the account of Jesus' rejection by His hometown of Nazareth. This chapter also describes the sending out of the twelve, and how these young babes in Christ were used by God to share His Word, minister in deliverance and release physical healing. The chapter continues with the sad story of the beheading of John the Baptist by a weak king, enslaved by lust and easily manipulated by others. Finally, there is a detailed narrative of the feeding of five thousand people with five loaves of bread and two fish. A group of people had converged on a spot by the Sea of Galilee from all the cities around, so eager to be with Jesus that they'd not thought to pack any food for themselves. When it was late in the day, the disciples realized that no one had any food so they suggested to Jesus that the people be sent away to find food for themselves in the surrounding villages. Jesus had a better idea!

The feeding of the five thousand is an amazing account. All ate *"and were filled"* by the five loaves and two fish as God multiplied it to meet the need, with twelve baskets of leftovers! God's faithfulness to provide superabundantly, liberally and without limitation is demonstrated here. His grace is not just minimally sufficient, but it is all sufficient for every need! He is Jehovah Jireh, whose resources are available to His children beyond what we can ask or even imagine (Ephesians 3:20).

After the miracle of feeding the five thousand, Jesus urged the disciples into a boat and sent them to the other side of the Sea of Galilee while He dispersed the crowds and then went off alone to pray. During the evening, a wind came up and He could see them straining against it. He left them to it, however, just as He often leaves us to strain for a while against the resistance we face. He knows that as we press against it, our spiritual muscles are developed. Later, He went walking on the sea towards the other side. When they saw Him, they thought He was some sort of ghost! He immediately reassured them, climbed into the boat and the wind ceased. The account says they were amazed beyond measurement *"for they had not understood about the loaves, because their heart was hardened"* (Mark 6:52).

One day when I was reading this passage, the last verse seemed to jump off the page at me. Mark is explaining that when the feeding of the five thousand happened earlier in the day, the disciples "did not get it". Before their very eyes they saw God's hand move to do a miracle, yet they were not impacted by it. They were so amazed when Jesus came walking on the water and stilled the storm because they had not understood any of what had happened earlier. It went right over their heads! They were unable to relate what Jesus had done in feeding the crowd to their own lives. They still did not understand who He was. The Scripture says this happened because their hearts were hard. The Greek word used conveys the picture of being covered over with a thick skin or hardened by a callus. By implication it means dull or dense.

Later, in Mark 8:17–21, Jesus again referred to their hard hearts. He had begun to warn them about the leaven of the Pharisees and that of Herod, the ungodly king. They thought that He was talking about their failure to bring more than one loaf of bread with them in the boat! Jesus, realizing they had no idea what He was talking about, then said to them,

"Why do you reason because you have no bread? Do you not yet perceive nor understand? **Is your heart still hardened?** *Having eyes, do you not see? And having ears, do you not hear? And do you not remember?"* (Mark 8:17–18)

He then goes on to remind them how many baskets of fragments were left over when He fed the five thousand and how many large baskets of leftovers were taken up when He fed the four thousand with seven loaves. He concludes with the question, *"How is it you do not understand?"* How could they think

He was worried about a lack of bread when they had just seen Him multiply a few loaves to feed thousands of people on two separate occasions? Again, He attributed their lack of understanding to their hard hearts. I believe this condition of hardness of heart affects God's people much more than we realize!

▶ *Hardness of heart is an insidious disease that leaves us spiritually crippled, unable to see or apprehend the reality of God's kingdom in our lives.*

The promise of new hearts

God promised in Ezekiel 36 that He would send the Holy Spirit and give His people new hearts,

> *"I will give you a new heart and put a new spirit within you; I will take the heart of stone out of your flesh and give you a heart of flesh."*   (Ezekiel 36:26–27)

He pledged back in the time of Ezekiel, 600 years before Christ, that He would take our hard hearts and do a divine exchange, replacing them with hearts softened by His hand.

I wondered why, then, did the disciples still have hard hearts? They had been walking with Jesus daily, spending the better part of every day being taught by Him. They went to sleep at night seeing Jesus' face. They woke up every morning in His presence. He spoke to them all day long. How could they still have hard hearts? So I asked the Lord about it. He explained to me that the Holy Spirit had not yet been poured out, a matter of importance because the promise of new hearts was tied to the promise of His Spirit. He also impressed upon me that at this point in their walk with Jesus, they were still following Him for what He could do for them. They thought they would have an exalted place in His kingdom when He saved them from the Roman government. They still did not understand who He really was, what He really came to do, or what the cost would be to follow Him. They were drawn to Him, and in awe of Him, but in many ways they were still serving themselves. Their commitment had not yet been hardened by life-transforming revelation or by the fires of affliction. Their time with Jesus was still just an exciting experience rather than a compelling commitment. His death and resurrection changed all that! What they only knew intellectually beforehand became a fire of revelation burning in their hearts. His death and resurrection, and the subsequent infilling of His Spirit, changed them from self-serving men who fled from Calvary for their own safety, to men who were willing to die for their faith. A divine exchange took place as the Holy Spirit filled them and did a work in their hardened hearts!

The condition of our hearts affects how we respond

Have you ever noticed what happens to something soft like butter when it is put under heat? It melts! But what happens when something that is hard, like clay, is heated by the sun? It gets even harder! I experienced this first hand growing up in the American state of Georgia. In the summer, the red clay soil would bake in the sun and contract, leaving the ground as hard as granite. We see this tendency of clay to harden under heat in the tableware that we use every day in our kitchens. The process of making pottery and china involves placing pieces of clay in a kiln where they are baked at very high temperatures. When the process is finished, we have dishes hard enough to use a knife on and resilient enough to be put in the hottest dishwasher! In the same way, hard hearts grow even harder when the heat and pressure of adversity is applied. Soft hearts simply melt and grow softer. This is why some people run *from* God when they hit rough spots and why other people run *to* God. It is also why adverse circumstances cause some people to become bitter, yet cause others to become more merciful and compassionate.

► *How we respond to adverse circumstances is all to do with the condition of our hearts!*

Allow me to share an example from my own experience. We have ministered to a number of people through the years who were severely physically and sexually abused as children. We had opportunity to pray with and minister to two women who had almost identical experiences in this regard, yet their responses to God were very different! One woman, even though she had been a Christian for a long time, was still hardened to God in many ways. She tended to blame Him and others for things rather than examining what part she might have had to play in what had happened. She had difficulty dealing with other people and was easily offended. Painful experiences caused her to become more bitter and mistrustful. She expected others to make room for her, rather than making room in her life for others. The other woman had been through the same kind of torture, degradation, and abuse. However, her heart would melt when God showed her something. She was usually quick to take responsibility for her sin, to repent and go to God with it. She asked forgiveness from others when she saw she'd been out of line. She wasn't perfect by any means, and she was not exempt from periods of rebellion and hopelessness, but her heart was almost always open for the Lord to bring correction and draw her back to Him. Why were their responses to God so different when they had been through the same awful experiences? The Lord showed us it all had to do with the nature and condition of their hearts.

▶ *Hard hearts not only get harder with heat and pressure, but it is only hard hearts that can break!*

The harder they are, the more brittle they become and the more easily they shatter when a blow is received. Soft hearts don't break when life deals us a resounding blow. They might be bruised and hurt for a while, but they do not break. Jesus came to heal our broken hearts (Luke 4:18), but He also sent His Spirit to change the condition of our hearts so that they need not break again! The more we allow the Holy Spirit to work the anointing oil from His throne into our hearts, the softer our hearts will become.

Unresolved hurt hardens hearts

Being Christians, even Spirit-filled ones, does not exempt us from hardness of heart. In fact, like the disciples, many of us are affected by this insidious disease and don't even realize it. It is probably a lot more common than we might have ever thought! Why is this?

I believe there is a common experience at the root of this condition. When we receive repeated spiritual or emotional hurts, or repeated disappointment, calluses begin to develop over our hearts if we are not careful to take these hurts and disappointments to the Lord. The Lord showed me this by talking to me about my feet! My feet are very callused from years of running around barefoot. In my twenties, I was *still* running barefoot – even over gravel and rocky places. He showed me that because my feet had experienced much abuse, my body formed calluses to protect the feet from more hurt.

To stop calluses from developing around our hearts, we must be willing to let go of all the self-pity, judgements and blame when we are hurt, and allow Him to bring immediate healing. The thick skin we develop over our hearts is a self-protection mechanism that belongs to our carnal human nature. It is the result of coping independently of God. Instead of finding our healing and our refuge in the Lord, looking to Him as our protector, we begin to try to take on that role and protect ourselves from more hurt.

Unfortunately, this thick skin or wall around our hearts does not bring healing and actually has an adverse affect in our lives, bringing even more hurt and disappointment! It affects our relationship with God and our relationship with other people. It leads to a lack of intimacy and sense of isolation and loneliness. It makes our hearts impervious so that Jesus' words of life cannot soak in. The result is that we become unable to receive teaching and unable to receive revelation understanding. Our spirits become dull and insensitive. It affects our discernment, our judgement, and our attitudes as well. We become critical and cynical, unable to feel God's compassion for others or His compassion for us.

This is the stony ground that Jesus spoke of in the parable of the sower (Matthew 13:20–21). The ground Jesus told of in this parable is the ground of our hearts. He is the sower, sowing His Word into our hearts. He passionately desires that it will fall on good ground so that it might bear much fruit in our lives. Jesus said anyone who has a hard or stony heart has *"no root"* and *"endures only for a while."* When the trials or the pressure comes, he *"stumbles."* The Greek suggests falling into a trap or being tripped up. Those with hard hearts are easily tripped up by offense. They are often shipwrecked by fear. Depression overpowers them. They can never hold their ground and are always up and down, blown off course by the winds of adversity because they are not rooted and grounded in Him.

Sin hardens hearts

> *"Therefore, as the Holy Spirit says:*
>
> *'Today, if you will hear His voice,*
> *Do not harden your hearts as in the rebellion,*
> *In the day of trial in the wilderness,*
> *Where your fathers tested Me, tried Me,*
> *And saw My works forty years.*
> *Therefore I was angry with that generation,*
> *And said, "They always go astray in their heart,*
> *And they have not known My ways."*
> *So I swore in My wrath,*
> *"They shall not enter My rest."' '*
>
> *Beware, brethren, lest there be in any of you an evil heart of*
> *unbelief in departing from the living God; but exhort one another*
> *daily, while it is called 'Today,'* **lest any of you be hardened**
> **through the deceitfulness of sin.***"*   (Hebrews 3:7–13)

Sin hardens us! Have you ever noticed that people who have led destructive lifestyles look very hard? One time at the end of a service, a woman brought another woman forward to be prayed over. I guessed the first woman's age at about 35 and the age of the second woman at about 60 years of age. I thought that perhaps this was a daughter bringing her mother forward for prayer. The Lord showed me that the second woman was not a Christian but that she was desperate and ready to open her heart to Him. I had the privilege of praying with her to receive Jesus into her heart and life. I found out later, however, that the "younger" woman was really 55 years old and the "older" woman, whom I mistakenly assumed might be her mother, was actually 20 years younger! She was a prostitute and a heroin addict, whose body was so ravaged and hardened by sin that she looked like an old woman.

In the Church world, I frequently see people hardened by other kinds of sin. Bitterness is the biggest culprit. Embittered people are easily recognizable because there is a certain hardness that shows even in their facial expressions. *Any* sin that is not confessed will open the door for spiritual death to work in our lives, resulting in hardness of heart. That is why it is so important for us to continually go before the Lord with repentant hearts, confessing our sin and receiving His cleansing. The Word of God does not promise that we will ever be totally free from sin as we walk on this earth. But it does offer a remedy for the sin that God is faithful to show us. In the first of his three epistles, John wrote, *"My little children, these things I write to you, so that you may not sin"* (1 John 2:1). In the same verse he goes on to tell us, however, that *"if anyone sins, we have an Advocate with the Father* [in the person of], *Jesus Christ"*. Notice he says *if* we sin, recognizing that we will. Let's be honest about our sin and put it under His blood, ensuring that our hearts stay soft before Him!

Jesus blamed divorce on hardness of heart

I heard some statistics recently that compared the divorce rates among Christians with those of the world in general. There was no significant difference! Jesus gives us some insight into why this is so in Mark 10:1–12. The Pharisees were testing Him, asking if it was lawful for a man to divorce his wife. He replied that divorce had been allowed under Moses, *but only because of the hardness of their hearts.* He went on to make it clear that divorce is not God's perfect plan for any couple. The Spirit-Filled Life Bible has an interesting commentary on the parallel account found in Matthew 19. It reads,

> "Jesus frankly addresses a pivotal issue: the cause of divorce is *hardness of heart.* Behind every broken marriage is a heart hardened against God, then hardened against one's mate ... The Devil will exaggerate your mate's failures and inadequacies, sow suspicion and jealousy, indulge your self-pity, insist that you deserve something better, and hold out the hollow promise that things would be better with someone else. But hear Jesus' words, and remember: God can change hearts and remove all hardness if we will allow Him."[1]

God specializes in changing hard hearts! The key, however, is allowing Him to do so. He waits for our invitation, as we ask Him to have His way in us regardless of the cost.

Trading the old for the new

The Lord spoke through the prophet Ezekiel to admonish His people,

> *" 'Cast away from you all the transgressions which you have committed, **and get yourselves a new heart and a new spirit**. For why should you die, O house of Israel? For I have no pleasure in the death of one who dies,' says the Lord GOD. 'Therefore turn and live!' "*   (Ezekiel 18:31)

How do we get ourselves a new heart? The Lord used an experience from my college days to answer this question for me. I worked one summer for the U.S. Fish and Wildlife Service at the Okefenokee Swamp in southern Georgia. Near where I worked there was a snake farm along one of the highways that was somewhat of a tourist attraction. As a farm girl I had grown up around snakes, but I was fascinated by the snakes at the roadside farm because there were a number of poisonous ones and they were huge! I stopped there several different times. Each time, there was at least one snake in the process of molting or shedding its skin. In this process, they would leave their hardened outer skin caught on a twig in the glass tank while they slithered off in their shiny new skin. It was interesting to me that the new skin was so much brighter, the colors so much richer and deeper than the old hardened skin. It was also softer to the touch. The old skins felt rough like sandpaper while the new ones were silky smooth. The Lord showed me one day that our hardness of heart is a lot like these old snakeskins in terms of how rough and ugly they are. Further, we can shed them just as easily if we submit to the work of His Spirit in our lives. We can exchange hearts covered in thick, self-protective skin for new soft hearts that are emblazoned with the brightness of His life and Spirit. James said we have not because we ask not (James 4:2). Have you asked Him for a new heart?

In *Voyage of the Dawn Treader*, from C.S. Lewis' Christian classic *The Chronicles of Narnia*, Eustace falls asleep in a dragon's lair and turns into a dragon himself. Later, after he has turned into a boy again, he recounts to Edmund how that happened. He explains how he was approached by the lion, Aslan, who led him to a pool of bubbly water and then told him to undress. He realized that as a dragon he had no clothes, so he began to scratch and dig at the hard, scaly skin that covered him. It peeled off, leaving another layer underneath, and another. But it was no good. Eustace could not shed himself of the hard, scaly dragon skin himself. There were just too many layers! The lion then told Eustace that it was something he, the lion, must do. Eustace recounts,

> "The first tear he made was so deep that I thought it had gone right into my heart. And when he began pulling the skin off, it hurt worse than anything I had ever felt . . . Well, he peeled the beastly stuff right off – just as I thought I had done myself the other three times, only they hadn't hurt – and there it was lying on the grass: only ever so much thicker, and darker, and more knobbly looking than the others had been."

He goes on to tell Edmund that after the lion pulled off the thick layers of dragon skin, he was again "smooth and soft as a peeled switch." The lion threw him in the bubbling water and after some time of swimming in this water, he realized that he was a boy again. The chapter finishes with the conclusion that from then on, Eustace was quite a different boy.[2]

When we allow the Lion of Judah to rip the layers of hardness off our hearts, our lives will be noticeably changed as well! But there are some principles found in this story that are important for us to understand as we seek the new soft hearts that God has for us. First, our own self-effort will never be enough to accomplish transformation. *Jesus* must do it. Secondly, His process does not always feel good. Many Christians run from anything that causes discomfort in their lives, operating under the misconception that anything that does not feel good cannot be God. How far this is from the truth! As the lion demonstrated in this story, God's deep work in our hearts is often painful. However, the end result is that we experience a new sense of freedom and purity. We can bask and frolic in the river of God with abandon when the weight of all that hardness of heart has been removed.

2 Corinthians 5:17 tells us,

> *"Therefore, if anyone is in Christ, he is a new creation; old things have passed away; behold, all things have become new."*

This promise describes part of our legal inheritance as children of light. Jesus paid for it and it is ours judicially or legally. However, it only becomes ours in experience as we work out our salvation, submitting all to Him. As we learn to abide in Him and exchange our hard hearts for His new ones, we become like Eustace – a new creation!

Prayer

Father, I confess to You that I still have hard places in my heart. I bring to You any hardness of heart and ask You to do a divine exchange. Please put a new heart and a new spirit within me! I want to trade my old hard heart for Your new soft one. I invite You to do a deep work of Your Spirit within me as I bring to You the sin that has hardened my heart. Wash me with Your blood, Lord Jesus, that I might be cleansed from all defilement of soul and spirit. I also bring to You all the hurts and disappointments that have caused my heart to grow hardened. Please forgive me for attempting to cope with hurtful situations on my own without You. Please forgive me for harboring unforgiveness, blame and judgements in my heart against other people and against You. Lord, I release and give to You any anger, bitterness, resentment or self-pity that I have been holding onto. I ask You to flood my heart now with Your healing love, even as I give and release these things to You. Dear Father, hold my broken and wounded heart in Your hands and make me whole again. Let the oil of Your Spirit infuse and transform my heart, bringing healing and softening. Transform me, Lord, into a new creation as I learn to abide in You and receive the new heart You have for me. Amen.

Notes

1. *The Spirit-Filled Life Bible*, Jack W. Hayford, General Editor (Thomas Nelson, Nashville, 1991), p. 1441.
2. C.S. Lewis, *The Chronicles of Narnia, The Voyage of the Dawn Treader* (Macmillan, New York, 1952), pp. 88–93.

Chapter 9

Going Deeper: the Art of Becoming a Living Sacrifice

We had a pastor many years ago who used to say, "The only problem with living sacrifices is that they keep crawling off the altar!" He was referencing Romans 12:1 which entreats,

> *"I beseech you therefore, brethren, by the mercies of God, that you present your bodies a living sacrifice, holy, acceptable to God, which is your reasonable service."*

The sacrifices required by God in the Old Testament were types and shadows of the sacrifice that would be made by Jesus Christ for us. However, some of them were *also* types or pictures of the spiritual sacrifices *we* are called to offer to God as His royal and holy priesthood (1 Peter 2:5, 9). We are called to offer spiritual sacrifices of praise (Psalm 69:30–31; Hebrews 13:15), joy (Psalm 27:6), brokenness and contrition of heart (Psalm 51:17), thanksgiving (Psalm 116:17), lifting of hands (Psalm 141:2) and material support (Philippians 4:16–18), as well as good works and communion with one another (Hebrews 13:16). However, the most significant spiritual sacrifice we are called to offer God is *ourselves*! He wants our hearts, our wills, our very lives – willingly dedicated and set apart to the King of kings and Lord of lords. Our former pastor was simply observing human nature when he commented upon our tendency to sidestep this level of consecration and commitment. Most of us *want* to be fully submitted to God, fully dedicated and given to Him. Yet, there is a part of us that also wants to run!

I remember one day when we lived in Plano, Texas. I was driving home from a particularly invigorating Christian meeting. The Lord had really been stirring my heart and drawing me to commit myself to Him in a deeper way. I remember praying all the way home, tearfully begging the Lord to take me to the cross and lay me on His altar. "I want to be crucified with Christ," I declared to Him, "so that it is no longer I who live, but Christ who lives in me!" The Apostle Paul's words were literally burning in my heart. I was so overcome by what God was doing in me that nothing else mattered. Nothing! All I wanted was to become more like Him and I was ready for Him to do whatever it would take. A week later, however, I found myself in desperate straits. It had been the week from hell. Everything that could have gone wrong went wrong. I came to a place where I was totally frazzled and worn down, so I went complaining to the Lord. After listening to me whine for a while, the Lord said very gently, "Dee, I am answering your prayer." I was thinking, "What prayer? I didn't ask for all this rubbish to happen to me!" He gently reminded me of the day I laid myself on His altar and begged Him to take me to the cross. How quickly I had forgotten! Not only that, when He began to answer the prayer, I was ready to run away! When He allowed the trials and tribulations into my life that would bring me to the end of myself and put to death my stinky flesh, all I could think about was how badly I wanted the situation to change!

Old Testament altars

The word "altar" in Hebrew is from a word meaning "sacrifice". An altar was simply a place of sacrifice. We find that altars were built throughout the record of the Old Testament. Noah built an altar after the floodwaters had receded and they were able to leave the ark (Genesis 8:20). Abram, later renamed Abraham by the Lord, built a number of altars (Genesis 12:6–7, 8; 13:1–4; 13:18; 22:9). Isaac, Jacob, Moses, and Gideon also built altars to the Lord. We find that an altar was often built as a point of contact when men were intensely seeking Him. When the Scripture says they *"called upon the name of the LORD there"*, the Hebrew paints a picture of them crying out to Him and accosting Him in prayer. Altars were also frequently built by the patriarchs to honor God following a life-changing encounter with Him. On a number of occasions, they named the place after Him in a way that was descriptive of how He had revealed Himself. For example, the names Jehovah Jireh ("The Lord Who Sees/Provides"), El Elohe Israel ("The Mighty God of Israel") Jehovah Nissi ("The Lord is My Banner"), and Jehovah Shalom ("The Lord is Peace"), are all names given to altars built by these patriarchs to describe the revelation of God that they received there. The Lord had promised them, *"In every place where I record My name I will come to you, and I will bless you"* (Exodus 20:24). His name was recorded at these altars so that the place would stand as a testimony of His presence and blessing in their lives. It was a place they could come back to at any time.

We have at least one recorded account of a patriarch returning to an altar that he had previously built. Abram went back to his altar between Bethel and Ai after the painful run-in with Pharaoh in Egypt (Genesis 13:1–4). Abram had lied to him in fear, telling him that Sarai was his sister when in actuality she was his wife. Pharaoh was extremely upset when he found out the truth and ran them out of Egypt. I think it likely that Abram returned to the last altar he had built in order to bring to the Lord the shame, guilt and turmoil surrounding his escapades in Egypt.

Altars were also built for other reasons. Joshua built an altar on Mount Ebal in obedience to the word of the Lord to Moses. Its purpose was primarily to honor God and to renew Israel's covenant with Him (Joshua 8:30–35). The people of Israel built an altar to the Lord during a time of great distress and travesty that affected the whole nation (Judges 21:1–4). Building an altar was their way of turning to the Lord in their grief.

A more permanent altar for blood sacrifice was included in the tabernacle that was built in the wilderness. The Lord gave Moses the exact specifications for it: the dimensions, materials to use, and design of it (Exodus 27). However, there was also a second altar in Moses' tabernacle. It was an altar of incense, which was placed just before the veil leading into the Holy of Holies where the presence of God dwelt. The Lord also gave exact specifications for the building of this altar (Exodus 30). Both of these altars were portable so that they could be carried around in the wilderness. Later, when the tabernacle of Moses was established at Shiloh in the promise land, they became permanent fixtures.

Even then, men of God still built their own altars to Him. Samuel built an altar to the Lord in his hometown of Ramah, from where he judged Israel most of his life (1 Samuel 7:15). Saul built altars to the Lord at different times (1 Samuel 14:35). David also built altars to the Lord. A very important one is recounted in 2 Samuel 24:18–25 (with a parallel account in 1 Chronicles 21:16–27). The Lord had sent a plague on Israel because of David's presumption in numbering the people. David pleaded with God to stop it, admitting his guilt and asking the Lord to put the weight of the judgement only upon him and his family. The Lord then sent a prophet to instruct David to build an altar on the threshing floor of Araunah (also known as Ornan), the Jebusite. Araunah wanted to give him the threshing floor and the oxen for the altar, but David insisted on paying for it, saying, *"nor will I offer burnt offerings to the* Lord *my God which costs me nothing"* (2 Samuel 24:24). He understood that an altar by its very nature is a place that costs us dearly! It is a place where we meet with God by giving something of ourselves to Him.

Types and shadows of what was to come

The altars built by the men of God in the Old Testament were made of earth (Exodus 20:22) or stone (Deuteronomy 27:2–8). The Lord directed that only whole or uncut stones be used in building altars. He explained, *"... for if you use your tool on it, you have profaned it"* (Exodus 20:25). Why would the Lord care? We see that it matters when we realize that the altars in the Old Testament were a foreshadowing of things to come on two different planes.

Firstly, the Old Testament altars were a type of the altars that we as new covenant people are to build with the rocky, hard issues of our lives. Geologists will tell us that there are three basic kinds of rocks: igneous, metaphoric and sedimentary. These rocks are all produced by different geological processes. Similarly, we have a variety of hard, rocky places in our lives, produced by different processes, but we can build altars with all of them! The Lord wants our hard issues "unhewn" or untouched by human hands because He wants us to bring these issues and situations to Him as they are, unpolluted by our interference and attempts to fix or sanctify things. As Sam Sasser, the renowned missionary and teacher, cautioned his students before he went to be with the Lord,

> "Don't change the shape of hard things. Don't reshape the story to make the hard things look like someone else's fault. Don't tool the difficulty, bring it in its original rough and rocky form to your altar."[1]

Secondly, as we offer our lives to the Lord in this way on our own altar, He then builds His heavenly altar out of us – His living stones. 1 Peter 2:5 ties together these living stones, which make a holy habitation for Him, with the kingdom of priests He has called to offer up spiritual sacrifices. We are concurrently the priests, the altar *and* the sacrifice – something that can only happen in the economy of God! The Old Testament altars were a type and shadow of the altar that sits before the throne of God (Isaiah 6:6; Revelation 6:8; 8:3; 9:13; 16:17). This is the one, made up of His living stones, on which we place ourselves as the living sacrifices Paul spoke of in Romans 12. He wants *us* unshaped and unpolluted by human interference as well. He wants us to come to Him just as we are, without masks and without any chisel of religiosity upon the sculpture of our lives.

The place of surrender

Altars are places of surrender.

▶ *Many of us have turmoil and tension in our hearts and in our lives because we are still fighting God.*

We are still kicking against what He is doing in our lives. There is still a horrendous internal conflict raging between our flesh and the Spirit of God within us. With surrender, however, comes peace! Building altars with the hard things in our lives opens the door for the peace of God to rule and reign in our hearts. There is a peace that comes from God's work in our lives and the righteousness it brings. Hebrews 12 admonishes us,

> "Now no chastening seems to be joyful for the present, but painful; nevertheless, afterward it yields the peaceable fruit of

righteousness to those who have been trained by it. Therefore
strengthen the hands which hang down, and the feeble knees, and
make straight paths for your feet, so that what is lame may not be
dislocated, but rather healed."   (Hebrews 12:11–13)

The lame places in our lives are healed as we bring them to the
Lord at an altar we have built, surrendering our thoughts,
feelings and pain to Him. There are many places of surrender,
many altars that the Lord challenges us to build throughout our
lives.

One significant place of surrender we all encounter is whether
or not we are going to continue serving Him when the going gets
rough. It's the place we come to when we make the decision that
once and for all, live or die, sink or swim we are going on with
God. Sometimes it takes a while to get there! I played around
with commitment to the Lord for eight years before I was ready
to make that decision. Afterwards, I was able to say that I had
only forward gears. Reverse had been stripped from my transmis-
sion by the altar I built one night in January 1982. That evening I
wrote a letter to the Lord and said to Him, "OK, I surrender! I give
up. I won't run from You anymore." Once we have gotten that
settled we sometimes think that is the end of it and that our walk
with the Lord will "just happen" now. We think we are sold out
to Him because we have built one altar and come to a place of
surrender. In actuality, we have merely come to the place where
the Lord can begin to work on our willingness to listen to His
voice and on our submission to Him in everyday things. He
brings many more opportunities to surrender and continue to
build altars!

The place of death

Psalm 116:15 tells us,

> *"Precious in the sight of the* LORD
> *Is the death of His saints."*

Altars are not just about surrender. They are also about death!
The sacrifices that were put on the altar in the Old Testament
were killed and then the fire from the altar burnt up all the flesh,

creating a *"sweet aroma to the Lord"* (Leviticus 1–3). Jesus' willing sacrifice of His own life for ours also brought forth a *"sweet-smelling aroma"* (Ephesians 5:2). God's altar is meant to be a place of death to our flesh – the place where we are crucified with Christ so that His life can become ours (Galatians 2:20). This is a different kind of death than the spiritual death that creeps into our lives through sin. This death to the flesh is a sweet smell to the Lord, and to the lost and dying world around us. Paul wrote to the church at Corinth,

> *"But thanks be to God, who ... through us spreads everywhere the fragrance of the knowledge of him. For we are to God the aroma of Christ among those who are being saved and those who are perishing. To the one we are the smell of death; to the other, the fragrance of life."*   (2 Corinthians 2:14–16, NIV)

▶   *The outworking of this **death-to-self process** in our lives is **freedom from bondage and freedom from sin**, that **nothing** might have dominion over us any longer except our Lord and King!*

Paul wrote to the Romans,

> *"What shall we say then? Shall we continue in sin that grace may abound? Certainly not! How shall we who died to sin live any longer in it? Or do you not know that as many of us as were baptized into Christ Jesus were baptized into His death? Therefore we were buried with Him through baptism into death, that just as Christ was raised from the dead by the glory of the Father, even so we also should walk in newness of life. For if we have been united together in the likeness of His death, certainly we also shall be in the likeness of His resurrection, **knowing this, that our old man was crucified with Him, that the body of sin might be done away with, that we should no longer be slaves of sin. For he who has died has been freed from sin."** (Romans 6:1–7)*

Building an altar with the hard, rocky issues of our lives and willingly placing ourselves upon His altar as a living sacrifice opens the way for the Lord to kill our carnal nature and bring us to a place where we are truly free to serve Him. Paradoxically in the kingdom of God, the way to life is through this death to self!

Jesus said, *"For whoever desires to save his life will lose it, but whoever loses his life for My sake will find it"* (Matthew 16:25). If we die, then we shall really live! So many of us are merely existing from one day to the next and calling it life. But it is not the abundant life Jesus came to bring. If we want that kind of life, there is a death that must take place – on His altar.

How to build an altar

Building an altar is simple, but not easy! In altar building, we come to the Lord in honesty and transparency, offering ourselves and our lives to Him. This sounds so simple, yet it can be the most difficult thing we have ever done! We offer Him the hard issues, the struggles, the painful situations, the hurts, the things we don't understand, the negative emotions, the ugly thoughts, the self-hate, the weaknesses and failings of our flesh and He touches them with the fire of His Spirit. Just as Isaiah's lips were touched with a coal from the heavenly altar and it brought cleansing (Isaiah 6:5–7), a new cleansing is brought in our lives as His fire touches us on the altar. Not everything we bring to the altar looks ugly, however. The Lord has required me to offer Him my natural strengths and abilities on the altar a number of times in the past. He wanted to crucify those things I was doing in my own strength, so that He could resurrect them in His power and with His anointing.

▶ *The important thing about building altars is that we leave there what we brought!*

So often, as our pastor friend commented, we crawl right back off the altar as soon as we have had our time with Him of renewed repentance or consecration. Or similarly, we pick back up the offenses or the hurts or the burdens that we took to the altar with us. All too often, we are careful to honor our word given to *people*, but we don't think twice about taking back something that we gave to the Lord! Why is that? Perhaps that is why numerous authors of the Old Testament books spoke of the fear of the Lord as the beginning of wisdom (Job 28:28; Psalm 111:10; Proverbs 1:7; 9:10). Maybe we do not have the healthy fear and reverential understanding of God's holiness and justice that we need to have. Maybe we do not understand either that when we break a vow to Him it opens a door for problems. Proverbs 20:25 (NIV) tells us,

> *"It is a trap for a man to dedicate something rashly and only later to consider his vows."*

Ecclesiastes 5:4–5 (NIV) cautions,

> *"When you make a vow to God, do not delay in fulfilling it. He has no pleasure in fools; fulfil your vow. It is better not to vow than to make a vow and not fulfil it."*

Violating our vows to the Lord may even open the door for curses to operate in our lives. The Lord told His people through the prophet Malachi that when they vowed to bring Him one thing and then substituted something different, it brought a curse (Malachi 1:14). We find that David and the other psalmists were very concerned with fulfilling any vows they had made to the Lord. It is a recurring theme throughout the book of Psalms.

▶ *I have found in my life that the more sensitive I have been to the Holy Spirit's nudge to build an altar, the closer I have gotten to receiving and walking in the inheritance the Lord has for me.*

Altars are a place of re-connection with God. In that sense, they are also a place of renewed connection with His grace, His spiritual provision and His plan and purpose for our lives. This re-connection brings us closer to tasting and experiencing the wealth of His kingdom that He purchased for us with His sacrificial death. Every altar made in our lives stands as a beacon radiating divine light, testifying of His power and blessing. Each one is a place to which we can return in the heat of battle, reunite with the God of the universe, and march forward again in His strength and anointing!

Prayer

Father, I desire to be that living sacrifice on Your altar. I don't want to wriggle off that altar or run away from the deep work You are trying to do in my life. I want to surrender! I submit my heart and my life to You fresh today, giving You permission to put to death my carnal nature that Christ might be revealed through my life in a more complete way. Lord, I want to build an altar today with the hard, rocky issues of my life. I bring them "unhewn" and free from my attempts to make them look better than they really are. I bring You the struggles, the painful situations, the hurts, the things I don't understand, the negative emotions, the ugly thoughts, the self-hate and my weaknesses in all their ugliness. Let us meet together over these things that have been stumbling blocks to me. Let the fire from heaven come and consume me, that I might become a sweet smelling savor to the world around me. I pray that You will reveal Yourself to me in a new way at this altar, just as You revealed Yourself to the patriarchs of the Old Testament at their altars. Lord, I want to know You more fully. Let this be a time of re-connection with You, that Your life and power might infuse and invigorate me in a fresh way. Strengthen me, I pray, that I might not take back what I have put on this altar and that I might not pull back from the work You are doing in my life. Amen.

Note
1. Dr. Sam Sasser, *The Priesthood of the Believer* (Fountain Gate Ministries, Plano, TX, no copyright date), p. 40.

Chapter 10

The Key
of Forgiveness

"I can't do it! I can't forgive him," the woman wailed. The person to whom she referred was one she held responsible for a great deal of hurt and pain in her life. What the person had done was clearly wrong. It had been utterly devastating to her and to others whom she cared about. Though she understood that she was called to forgive, she felt that the depth of the pain experienced at this person's hands justified her unforgiveness. Further, she felt that she was unable to forgive. The pain just went too deep. In reality, however, her refusal to forgive was *holding in* the pain, keeping it intact and causing the wounding to stay fresh and unhealed. This precious woman of God was tormented by the anger and bitterness that continually rose up when she thought about this person or what had happened. Her unforgiveness was destroying *her* life, not the other person's!

This scenario is replayed on a daily basis around the world and throughout the Body of Christ. After years of counseling people, Dave and I have come to the conclusion that unforgiveness is the single most powerful source of captivity in the Body of Christ. In fact, our general observation has been that the more oppressed someone is, the more unforgiveness they are probably harboring. Learning to walk in our inheritance, free from the captivity of the enemy in our lives, necessitates a deeper understanding of forgiveness and a willingness to embrace forgiveness as an attitude and a lifestyle.

In the gospel of Matthew, Jesus said to Peter,

> *"I will give you the keys of the kingdom of heaven, and whatever you bind on earth will be bound in heaven, and whatever you loose on earth will be loosed in heaven."*   (Matthew 16:19)

When He appeared to the disciples after the resurrection, He commissioned them to be sent out as His ambassadors and then made this curious statement,

> *"If you forgive the sins of any, they are forgiven them; if you retain the sins of any, they are retained."*   (John 20:23)

Forgiveness is one of the keys to the kingdom. There is a binding and loosing dynamic involved in it. The Greek word translated "retain" in John 20:23 means "to take possession of or continue to hold onto something". It is a picture of binding something to oneself. It actually comes from a root word that speaks of power or dominion. We want to hold onto our unforgiveness because we think it gives us power over someone else. Instead, in the paradoxical nature of the kingdom, it gives sin power over us! When we bind people by not forgiving them here on earth, we place spiritual shackles upon them, but even bigger spiritual shackles upon ourselves! As we loose people from our unforgiveness, the spiritual bondages are then loosed in the heavenly realm. Not only that, but Jesus said that through our forgiveness, others' sins can be *"remitted unto them"* or *"forgiven them"* (John 20:23). This means that as Christ's ambassadors here on earth, we have His delegated authority to forgive people their sins on His behalf. We can speak forgiveness and blessing over people as His representatives, releasing them from the guilt and burden of their sin. This is a privilege extended to every member of the Body of Christ.

The importance of forgiveness

Many of us know that forgiveness is important and that we are called to forgive, but we don't fully understand why. Personally, I find it very difficult to embrace something when I don't understand why it is necessary. I just never make the effort! Walking in forgiveness is important for several reasons.

First, it is a prerequisite to our receiving the Father's forgiveness for our own sin. Jesus said in Matthew 6:

> *"For if you forgive men when they sin against you, your heavenly Father will also forgive you. But if you do not forgive men their sins, your Father will not forgive your sins."*
> (Matthew 6:14–15, NIV)

In Mark 11, He said it this way,

> *"And whenever you stand praying, if you have anything against anyone, forgive him, that your Father in heaven may also forgive you your trespasses. But if you do not forgive, neither will your Father in heaven forgive your trespasses."*   (Mark 11:25–26)

Secondly, unforgiveness opens the door for torment and captivity in our lives. In Matthew 18 we find the parable of the unmerciful servant. It is really a story about forgiveness. Jesus told this story after Peter had asked Him about God's view on forgiveness. In this parable, the master forgave one of his servants a debt. This same servant then refused to release another servant from *his* debt (a smaller debt at that) and had him thrown in prison. When the master heard about it, he was understandably upset and had the unforgiving servant given over to the tormentors. Jesus concluded the parable with this statement:

> *"This is how my heavenly Father will treat each of you unless you forgive your brother from your heart."*
> (Matthew 18:35, NIV)

Thirdly, we find that walking in forgiveness is a condition for prevailing prayer. Not forgiving, to put it plainly, is sin. *Any* sin acts as a barrier and a block to answered prayer (Isaiah 59:2). It also opens the door for spiritual death to begin to work in our lives, quenching the life that Jesus came to bring (Romans 6:16, 23; James 1:15).

Lastly, in the gospel of Luke, we find even more said about forgiveness. Luke records Jesus as saying,

> *"Judge not, and you shall not be judged. Condemn not, and you shall not be condemned.* **Forgive, and you will be forgiven.** *Give, and it will be given to you: good measure, pressed down, shaken together, and running over will be put into your bosom.* **For with the same measure that you use, it will be measured back to you."**   (Luke 6:37–38)

We see a spiritual principle highlighted in these verses. We get what we give. If we sow forgiveness, we will reap forgiveness! That was really Jesus' point in the parable of the unmerciful servant. Our Father will have mercy and forgive us *as* we have mercy and forgive others. Not only that, we will reap forgiveness in our relationships with other people. If we are merciful, people will be merciful to us. If we walk in judgement, we will be held up in judgement.

I remember a situation I was in a number of years ago. I was so upset with a certain person about what they had done that I couldn't seem to muster the motivation to let go of it. I wanted to see justice done. The Lord quietly whispered to me one day, "Dee, you have a choice here. You can release the judgement, extend mercy and consequently keep yourself in a place to receive My mercy. Or you can hold onto the judgement and reap judgement in your own life. Which do you want?" I decided I would rather have the mercy!

Walking in forgiveness is also important for our physical and emotional health. A root of bitterness will grow out of the soil of unforgiveness. If left unchecked, it will grow into a tree that yields the fruit of anger, frustration, resentment, negativity and depression, just to name a few things! At least one scientific study has linked bitterness to a higher incidence of heart attacks. A recent *Reader's Digest* article referred to a study conducted by Hope College in Holland, Michigan. When asked to remember a past hurt, those tested recorded "steep spikes in blood pressure, heart rate and muscle tension." The article also quoted a test conducted by Stanford University Psychologist Fred Luskin on five women from Northern Ireland whose sons had been murdered. After undergoing a week of forgiveness training, the women's sense of hurt, measured using psychological tests, *fell by more than half.* The study found they were also less likely to feel depressed or angry.[1] Others in the medical community suspect that unforgiveness and bitterness also lead to ulcers, colonitis, and digestive problems. Our spiritual well-being is interconnected with our emotional and physical well-being. Unforgiveness will affect every area of our lives!

Forgiveness and physical healing

One of the students at our ministry training center shared with us a beautiful story of how forgiveness made way for a miraculous healing in her life. Danni[2] had been physically abused by her father as a child, a fact known to, but ignored by, her mother. She then married a man who also abused her. He was extremely violent – threatening her with a gun, attempting to strangle her and even breaking her fingers at different times. He threatened to kill her, cut her up into little bits, and bury the pieces in the garden. She suffered severe mental torture as well as physical abuse at his hands. Then when she was in her early 20s, a doctor dropped the bombshell that she also had a sexually transmitted disease that had been given to her by her husband. She was told at the time that this STD was responsible for her inability to get pregnant and have a family, something she had longed for since her teenage years. She finally escaped from her violent husband, and was taken in by a Christian couple who nurtured her back to health. Through much prayer and counseling, she came through it all. "But," she confided, "the cloud of not being able to have children was overpowering."

After meeting and marrying her present husband, a lovely Christian man, she was still unable to get pregnant. When she finally did, it always resulted in a miscarriage. She was told that both the infertility problem and the inability to carry a baby for any length of time were related to the sexually transmitted disease given to her by her previous husband. She believes now, however, that there were some spiritual issues hindering her as well. Looking back on it, she feels that her womb had been "closed up" by a number of things. She relates that her life was taken over by fear, and that she felt unworthy and undeserving to have children. She also came to see, after many years of anguish, that the lack of forgiveness towards her ex-husband and towards her parents was a major hindrance to her physical health and ability to have children. She saw more clearly the bitterness, the hardness of heart, the hatred and the hurt that had built up inside of her as a result of not forgiving. Danni eventually came to a place where the Lord showed her that she could not move forward until she forgave. He encouraged her to press through the pain and choose to forgive her parents and finally her ex-husband. She soon became pregnant.

Danni had been told by experts, long before this pregnancy happened, that there was no hope. She had gone through three IVF treatments, suffered nine miscarriages and experienced fifteen years of anguish in her inability to have children. However, the Lord had encouraged her through the years to believe Him and trust Him for children. He had even specifically promised her in 1992 that He would give her a daughter. The Lord sustained her with prophetic words like the one through a visiting minister in which He spoke, "What looks dead is alive, and I am going to bring it forth because I am a faithful God." He encouraged her by His Spirit to pray over her own womb and the children it would bring forth.

▶   *Yet nothing happened until she was able to forgive those who had traumatized and almost destroyed her.*

On the 31st August, 1995, little Jasmine,[3] the promise of God, was born to proud and thankful parents. The medical community described her birth as a miracle. It was. Her birth was also a testimony of the healing power of forgiveness!

The nature of forgiveness

We have found that many Christians have some misconceptions about forgiveness that hinder or block their choice to forgive. Many mistakenly believe that to forgive means we are condoning what happened to us. In abuse situations particularly, this misconception keeps many precious children of God from being able to forgive. Forgiving does not mean that what was done was OK! It only means we are willing to hand the person over to the Lord and put them in His hands for judgement rather than continuing to hold onto the judgement ourselves. We have many other misconceptions about forgiveness that may need to be exposed and adjusted:

- Forgiveness is *not* tolerance or diplomacy. It is *not* wavering in our convictions about right or wrong. We can stand firmly for integrity yet still walk in forgiveness.

- Forgiveness is *not* forgetting. We can forgive but still remember what happened. However, once the forgiveness process is complete, the painful "sting" will be gone in our memory of what happened.

- Forgiveness is *not* looking the other way. It is *not* a passive non-response. We can acknowledge that what was done was vindictive, selfish or hurtful, but still forgive it.

- Forgiveness is *not* the same as feeling healed of the hurt. Healing will often come later, after we have made the choice to forgive.

- Forgiveness is *not* an event. It does not happen suddenly all at once.

- Forgiveness is *not* extended because people deserve it. They rarely do. We rarely deserve forgiveness either!

- Forgiveness is *not* impossible. All of us can forgive through the strength and enabling that the Lord provides. He does not call us to do anything that He will not grace us to do.

What is forgiveness then? How does it really work? Forgiveness is a *process* that is *initiated* by a deliberate act of the will when we *choose* to forgive someone. It is an attitude of the heart that flows into an action.

▶ *Forgiveness is the process whereby we choose to release others from our penalty or judgement and place them in God's hands. It is releasing them from any debt we feel they owe us or others, in the same way our heavenly Father has released us from the debt we owed Him when we sinned against Him.*

Though forgiveness is not a feeling, opening the door for the process of forgiveness to work in our lives will lead to a sense of greater peace and well-being.

Another way we could define forgiveness would be this way:

▶ *Forgiveness is granting pardon to an offending person.*

Forgiveness is offered not because the other person deserves it, but in obedience to God. If we wait to forgive until people deserve it, we will never experience the freedom and blessing that comes into our lives through forgiveness! We will continue to miss out on experiencing the fullness of the inheritance that the Lord has purposed for us.

A real-life pardon!

Before my husband Dave came to know the Lord, he slid heavily into drugs and the party lifestyle. When I met him he was a typical pothead with a guitar and a motorcycle. My dad once referred to him as a "subdued, partially-matured hippy". Dave and I had quite a laugh about that for many years! But there was one thing about Dave's life at that time which was not so humorous. He was arrested and convicted of possession of marijuana "with intent to distribute" in 1978. It meant he was viewed as a drug dealer. Though in the end he was not sent to prison, he walked away from this ordeal with a record as a convicted felon, resulting in the removal of several of his citizenship rights. After the conviction he was not allowed to vote, run for public office or own a firearm. Further, he was required to reveal on every job application, if it were asked, that he was a convicted felon. It was intended that he would bear the penalty for his guilt the remainder of his lifetime. Then in the early 1990s we found out that the Governor of New Mexico was offering pardons to many whom had been convicted of drug offenses earlier in their lives. Dave applied for a pardon, and on December 4, 1994 he received a full pardon and restoration of all citizenship rights lost at the time of his conviction. The pardon wiped his slate clean. It was as if the felony conviction had never happened! He was promised that all computer records of his offense would be purged. The paper he received, signed by the Governor of the state, reads in part, "the sentence of the person has been fully discharged". His guilt was forgiven and his sin covered by the pardon. He did not necessarily deserve it, but mercy was extended to him. Dave walked away free to go on with his life without the stigma of that judgement against him. This is what happens when we forgive or pardon people for their offenses against us. Consequently, as we have seen from looking at God's Word, it also releases the Father to extend mercy and pardon to us!

Forgiveness flows in three directions

There are three areas in which we must learn to walk in forgiveness in order for God's inheritance to become a reality in our lives. The first and most obvious one concerns forgiving other people. These are the people who have abused, rejected, abandoned, ignored or offended us. It will include the people who falsely accused or betrayed or lied to us. The list of people we need to forgive also includes the ones who called us names or made fun of us. Parents who did not protect us or who did not do a very good job of parenting also need to be on this list. It will include all the people who have misunderstood us or attributed motives to us that were not ours. To sum up, our forgiveness should incorporate anyone who has hurt us, or our loved ones, in any way. Sometimes it is much easier for us to forgive those who hurt us personally, but because we feel so protective of the ones we love, it is very difficult to forgive anyone who hurt *them.*

The second area where forgiveness needs to flow is towards God. Many of us have a hard time with the thought of forgiving God because it means admitting we have been angry with Him or have been holding something against Him. The silly thing about our reluctance is that He already knows! He is omniscient. We can't keep anything hidden from Him! A religious spirit often rises up, however, and whispers to us, "You can't admit you were angry with *God!*" Irrationally, we find ourselves waiting for the lightning bolt to strike us dead on the spot. Not only does He know all about how we feel, but the Creator of the universe is big enough to handle one of His kids being angry with Him. It won't knock Him off His throne! It is important for us to get honest with the Lord about how we have felt and release Him from the judgements we held against Him when He didn't do things the way we expected or thought He should, when He allowed things to happen that hurt us, or when He didn't seem to be there when we needed Him.

▶ *Disappointment with God can be a subtle trap that the enemy uses to embroil us in a quicksand of resentment, unforgiveness and bitterness.*

We must give the Lord the liberty to do things His way, not our way, knowing that He can see the end from the beginning. It is also imperative that we trust Him, knowing that He has our best interests in mind even when we don't understand why things are happening the way they are. When we find ourselves disappointed with the Lord, it's time to go straight to Him with that disappointment, put it in His hands, and release Him from any judgements we have begun to pick up towards Him. We can also pray for grace to trust Him more!

The third area of forgiveness is towards ourselves. It is the most overlooked area of forgiveness and often the hardest of all! Even when we see the importance of forgiving others and releasing the Lord from any judgements against Him, we often think we have a right to hold onto not forgiving ourselves – because it is *us*! However, the principle is the same regardless of who stands as the object of our unforgiveness. If there is *any* lack of forgiveness in our hearts, our heavenly Father won't forgive us. We must release ourselves from this unforgiveness and self-condemnation or we will never walk free to receive the fullness of our godly inheritance. Again, forgiving ourselves does not mean we gloss over our failures or pretend that we did nothing wrong. We can walk in honesty and humility, fully recognizing our weaknesses and failings, but still extend mercy to ourselves in obedience to the Lord's directives. We can go to Him and confess our sin to Him without continuing to beat ourselves up and hate ourselves for blowing it. We can give the judgement we have been holding against ourselves to Him, allowing *Him* to be the Judge in our lives.

Roslyn's testimony – the victory that forgiveness brings

A recent British *Daily Mail* headline trumpeted the news, "One in 20 Women are Rape Victims".[4] According to the article, shocking new statistics have revealed that there are three-quarters of a million victims of rape in England and Wales, an area not much larger than the state of Florida. Roslyn[5] is one of these women. She was only thirteen years old when she was raped by an older "friend of a friend" who had kindly offered to give her a lift home. He pulled over on an isolated stretch of road where there was no traffic, and proceeded to attack her, ripping away her childhood, her innocence and her personhood in a nightmare that seemed to destroy her life. Roslyn was never able to tell anyone what happened, for fear of being blamed. She knew he would deny it and she was sure everyone would believe him. She envisioned the accusations, the ugly innuendoes and the quiet whispers that would be slyly made in dark corners around the community. She could anticipate the hot shame and embarrassment she would feel if everyone knew what had happened to her. It was more than she could bear. So she kept silent and carried the pain alone. To this day, her family still does not know.

Roslyn shares that she went straight into the bathtub and scrubbed herself raw, but nothing would take away the sense of defilement. She continued to feel dirty and worthless as the years went by. She felt she must have somehow deserved what had happened. She says, "He not only raped me, he took my life from me. I'd have been better off if he killed me." Despite becoming a Christian later as a teenager, she still felt she would be better off dead. She attempted suicide at age 17, but her life was spared, and she continued on in abject misery. She was not able to trust people or be vulnerable, building a hard shell of self-protection around herself so that she could never be raped again, literally or figuratively.

Even as an adult, she was always careful to avoid going anywhere near where the rape had taken place for fear that something else would happen to her. She would drive miles out of her way to studiously avoid it. Twenty-one years after the rape, however, she was forced to drive by the spot because of road construction. She confides that she "freaked out" and totally panicked. That was when she knew it was time to do something about the rape and its affect on her life.

As a Christian, she understood that she needed to forgive the man who had raped her. She chose to forgive him, but it only went as deep as she knew how to go at that point. "It was pretty surface," she says, "because there was still a lot of anger, bitterness and a desire for vengeance going on inside of me." Still, just making *the choice* to forgive him made things easier and lifted some of the burden off of her. She says she noticed that the power he had over her diminished considerably. But other repercussions of the rape were operative in her life, gnawing away at her inside. She still felt dirty. She continued to feel like an empty "non-person" devoid of all value.

Then a few years ago, she had the opportunity to go through some counseling that radically changed her life. The counselors were able to help her come to a deeper place of forgiveness towards the man who had so violated not only her womanhood, but her personhood. She was also able, for the first time, to *forgive God* for allowing it to happen. She was further able to *forgive herself* for holding onto the anger and the bitterness, and to *receive His forgiveness* for holding onto these things. Finally, she asked the Lord where He was when it happened. She explains, "What He showed me just totally blew me apart. God was there! He was grieving over what was happening and was hurting as much as I was. It released me. I could see I wasn't on my own."

As the forgiveness and the healing began to unlock things within her, she realized for the first time that the Lord could remove her shame and that she need not stay bound by the effects of what had happened all those years before. She also realized, however, that He could not free her from the fallout until she let go of those things and allowed Him to do so. She took the plunge and released everything to Him, receiving what the Lord had for her instead. She says of this moment, "It was incredible! I felt like I had been washed from the inside out."

Some time later, Roslyn discovered the depth of the victory God had wrought in her life. Driving with a friend one day, they passed by the very spot where the rape had happened. Clumps of holly were growing on the spot, and her friend wanted to stop and pick some to take home to use in a flower arrangement. Roslyn was able to get out of the car and walk around, treading over the *very ground* where the devastation in her life had taken place. It was a fulfillment of God's promise, *"Every place that the sole of your foot will tread upon I have given you"* (Joshua 1:3). Roslyn knew at that moment that she was truly forgiven, healed and clean. She was free! It was finally settled in her heart that she was no longer a worthless nothing, but a *real person* – saved, anointed and appointed by God for such a time as this. Victory was hers!

The challenge we face

Many of us have not experienced the same depth of trauma as Danni and Roslyn. Yet we can be similarly bound by unforgiveness. The justification that we each offer will be different, but the shackles we place upon ourselves are the same. We can find a new place of liberation in our lives by choosing to forgive and let go of all judgement and bitterness. As we do, we will discover an open door to more of our godly inheritance!

Prayer

Lord, I desire to answer Your call to forgive today. I choose to forgive each person who has knowingly or unknowingly hurt me or those I love in any way, whether they deserve it or not. I recognize that in choosing to forgive them, I am not condoning what they did. Rather, I am simply choosing to let go of my judgement against them and put them into Your hands for You to judge as You see fit. I recognize that as I extend mercy and forgiveness, I will likewise receive mercy and forgiveness. I choose to let go of the hatred, anger, bitterness and resentment that I have harbored towards these people. I put these emotions that have poisoned my soul into Your hands, Lord. I don't want to hold onto them anymore. I don't want to harbor them anymore, allowing them to be a substitute source of comfort. *You* want to be my comfort and the one I find solace in – not the anger, resentment and bitterness. As I make the choice today, Lord, I ask that You would take the forgiveness process deeper in me until its work is complete. I also ask You to bring the healing I need to every place of wounding represented by the unforgiveness in my life. Touch those places I pray, with Your hand, and reveal Yourself to me in a fresh way as my Jehovah Rapha, the Lord Who is My Healer.

I choose today to forgive You, Lord, for anything I have held against You. I choose to release You from every judgement I made against You when You didn't do things my way or when You allowed things to happen in my life that I didn't understand. Lord, I choose to trust You even when I don't understand why these things happened. I want every barrier to come down between us so that I can turn to You in the midst of any pain and devastation, to find my comfort, my security and my hope in You.

I also choose to forgive myself today for continuing to relive and replay in my mind the hurtful things that were said and done, stirring up the unforgiveness towards others within me. I choose to forgive myself for holding onto any anger, bitterness, resentment or hatred and for looking to those things to comfort me in my pain. I also choose to forgive myself for the mistakes I have made, for the times I have stumbled and for every misjudgement that caused harm to those I love. I extend mercy to myself. I place myself in Your hands for You to be my Judge, Lord.

Finally, Father, I receive Your forgiveness – for harboring unforgiveness and bitterness towards others, and for any vindictiveness or desire for revenge which I have embraced. I willingly confess my sin. Thank You for Your cleansing and Your forgiveness, Lord (1 John 1:9). I also receive Your forgiveness for any way I have inflicted hurt on others out of my own hurt. I pray that You will cover my mistakes, dear Father, and in Your grace bring healing and restoration – not only to myself, but to others who have been affected by the corrupting power of unforgiveness in my life. Let Your kingdom come more fully in my life as I learn to use the key of forgiveness. Amen.

Notes

1. *Readers' Digest* (Pleasantville, NY, April 2002), p. 173.
2. Name has been changed to protect privacy.
3. Name has been changed to protect privacy.
4. The *Daily Mail*, Tuesday July 23, 2002, p. 1.
5. Name has been changed to protect privacy.

Chapter 11

Liar, Liar, Pants on Fire!

The story of Charles Blondin's walk over Niagra Falls provides a good illustration of the difference that exists between what we think we believe and the inward belief system that dictates our attitudes and actions. I have heard that Blondin walked a tight-rope over Niagra Falls many years ago, awing the crowds with his performance. He then amazed them even more, however, by suggesting he could walk the tightrope over the falls carrying another person on his back. He asked the crowd, as the story goes, "Do you believe I can do it?" at which point the crowd went wild, responding back, "We believe it!" Then Blondin asked, "Which of you will be that person?" A hush fell over the crowd. They avoided looking at one another and shuffled in nervous silence. No one stepped forward. Finally, Charles Blondin's manager volunteered. The crowd was quick to acknowledge that Blondin could accomplish such a great feat, until it came time to act on what they said they believed. Then each realized that what they thought they believed and what they actually believed in their hearts were very different! None believed enough to risk his or her own life. Most Christians are like Blondin's crowd in many respects. When we come to know the Lord, we want to believe what He says is true. We try hard to believe it, often convincing ourselves that we really *do* believe it. However, when the time comes to put our lives on the line, we find out that our actions are governed by thoughts and attitudes that are contrary to what God says He can do or what He says is true. Deep down, our thinking is quite different from His!

Our thinking needs an overhaul!

One of Jesus' primary messages throughout the gospel accounts was, *"Repent for the kingdom of heaven is at hand"* (Matthew 4:17). As mentioned in an earlier chapter, the word translated "repent" is the word *metanoeo* in the original language of the New Testament. It literally means "change your mind" or "change the way you think".

▶ *Jesus suggested that it is necessary for us to change our thinking before we can understand or apprehend His kingdom for ourselves.*

Later, the Apostle Paul wrote that we are transformed by the renewing of our minds (Romans 12:2). Renew means to be made new again or to return something to its original state. What was the original state of our minds? Before sin entered the world at the fall, humankind was in the image and likeness of God. Our minds were pure, undefiled and uncorrupted by sin or by the deception of Satan, called the god of this world in the Scriptures. God wants to restore and renew our minds and our thinking to this state of purity and wholeness that reflects His nature, character, will and purposes. That is why He has purchased for us, by the blood of His Son, *the mind of Christ* (1 Corinthians 2:16). Legally, it is ours. However, there is a process through which we must walk whereby it becomes ours more and more in experience. A divine exchange must take place in our thinking – our corrupted junk for His pure treasure! Jesus Christ was a perfect reflection of the Father on this earth. Similarly, our lives, including our thinking, are meant to demonstrate Jesus to the world around us. As the Lord works in us to conform us to His image, our minds are renewed more completely and we are able to increasingly exhibit the mind of Christ.

Until we repent or change the way we think, allowing His salvation to be worked out in that area of our lives, our belief system is still carnal and contrary to His. This internal belief system has been shaped by many factors. Firstly, it has been shaped by the experiences we have had. For example, if we have been abandoned by others in our hour of need, we begin to form a belief about other people. This belief may be that they are only concerned for themselves, cannot be trusted and will always abandon us. Words spoken over us also shape what we think. If we have been told we are stupid all of our lives, chances are we will think of ourselves that way! Our family heritage and the environment in which we were raised also contribute to shaping our internal belief system. For example, those who are raised in a family that was not close often internalize the message that they are all alone and must go through life independent of help from others. It makes sense to them because this has been their experience. Finally, our carnal nature also determines much of what we still believe in our hearts. Our natural man does not understand the things of the Spirit of God (1 Corinthians 2:14). It has been molded by sin, selfishness, pride and independence. It is the part of us that is still untouched by the regenerating power of God. Though we might wish otherwise, our carnal nature still shapes a portion of our thinking and internal belief system.

We sometimes speak out of this internal belief system, especially in times of stress. When our guard is down, what bursts out of our mouths is frequently an indication of what we are *really* believing in our hearts. Jesus explained that out of the abundance of the heart the mouth speaks (Luke 6:45). There have been many times through the years when, despite how much I wanted to believe God, what came out of my mouth was fear, hopelessness or negativity of some sort. I found myself saying things like "It's never going to happen"; "The situation is hopeless"; "I can't do this"; "You can't trust anyone" or the fear-revealing words, "But what if . . ." Such remarks can reveal the huge disparity between our internal belief system and our theology. I was very clear on what I believed theologically. However, in times of testing and stress, I found I was living out of something very different in my heart! I discovered that my understanding of God and His Word was frequently still theoretical or intellectual, and had not yet invaded and transposed my internal belief system.

For example, even as a very young Christian I knew that the Lord promises to provide for us and take care of our every need if we put Him first. If anyone had asked me if I were trusting God for our provision, I would have said, "Of course!" However, I worried about money all the time. I rewrote our budget continually, concerned about whether we would have enough to pay the upcoming bills. We had two young children who drank a lot of milk, so I watered it down to stretch it farther. I remember saving for months for a $5 pair of sunglasses and being devastated when they fell on the pavement and were scratched. I was so upset because I *knew* it would be ages before I could afford another pair. I really did not believe that the Lord would provide for our needs. What I believed in my heart was that I would be abandoned, that I was not worth the Father's care and blessing, and that I could not depend on or trust anyone except myself. I found it difficult to reconcile the facts of my past experience with God's truth. I had been believing the enemy's lies for so long that I did not know how to live any differently.

Sowing and reaping – life or death

We often do not realize that when we believe Satan's lies, we are actually in agreement with him. This agreement constitutes a form of covenant, binding us to the enemy and giving him a legal right to harass and torment us. God's people in the Old Testament were told to make no covenant with the enemy (Deuteronomy 7:2). However, we do it all the time as we come into agreement with the devil and yield to his lies!

The Lord blew my mind one day as I was reading through the gospel of Matthew. Chapter 18:19 reads,

> *"I say to you if two of you agree on earth concerning anything that they ask, it will be done for them by My Father in heaven."*

The Holy Spirit nudged me very hard at that point to get my attention. Then He said to me, "The two do not have to be two *people* you know." I had no idea what He was getting at so I asked Him, "What do you mean?" He replied, "You can agree with Me or you can agree with the devil. It is still two agreeing." I can agree with the devil who tells me I am alone and abandoned or I can agree with God who tells me in His Word that He will never leave me or forsake me, that He is *for* me, and that He holds me in His hand. My agreement with the devil forms a covenant with him that opens a door for him to work in my life, bringing to pass the very things that I fear. If my agreement is with God, however, it establishes covenant with Him and opens the door for His grace and power to flow freely in my life. Our thinking and its effect in our lives provides another example of the principle of sowing and reaping.

▶ *We are sowing thoughts, and depending on who those thoughts are in agreement with, we will reap either life or death!*

When Dave and I were in Bible College, one of our professors shared with us the following maxim that I have remembered through the years:

Sow a thought, reap an action;
Sow an action, reap a habit;
Sow a habit, reap a character;
Sow a character, reap a destiny.

Most of us believe there can be no harm in our thoughts or what we think. We believe that all of our thoughts are neutral, as long as we are not acting on them. But this is a lie in itself. It is exactly what our enemy wants us to believe so that we will ignorantly continue in agreement with him! Jesus illustrated the potential power of harm in our thoughts in Matthew 5:28. He pointed out that if a man lusts after a woman, entertaining thoughts of illicit activity with her, he has already committed the action of adultery with her in his heart. Similarly, the Apostle John equated thoughts of hatred towards one's brother with the action of murder (1 John 3:15). While most of our thinking may not be quite as extreme as lust or hatred, we cannot refute the principle that there is power in our thoughts and attitudes – for good or for evil. We will reap what we sow.

The impact of believing the lies

We may divide those things that are part of our internal belief system into two categories – beliefs that are either godly or ungodly. Counselors Chester and Betsy Kylstra, authors of the counseling manual *Restoring the Foundations*, define ungodly beliefs as "all beliefs, decisions, attitudes, agreements, judgements, expectations, vows and oaths that do not agree with God (His Word, His nature, His character)". Similarly, the Kylstras define godly beliefs as those that *do* agree with God's Word, nature and character.[1] Godly beliefs also agree with His eternal purposes for us.

The devil is the father of lies and the truth is not in him. His lies are calculated to kill us, steal from us and destroy every good thing in our lives. When we believe them, we open the door for spiritual death and destruction to overshadow the life that Jesus came to bring us. What happens to us when we believe the enemy's lies? Here are just a few things that can happen:

- Our relationships with God and other people are hindered.
- Our perception of things are distorted – they seem much bigger or worse than they really are.
- Release of God's blessing in our lives is blocked.
- We are locked into a coffin of death, unable to fulfill the plan and purpose God has for our lives.
- The door is opened for demonic oppression.
- We become prisoners of unhealthy patterns.
- Our faith gets short-circuited.

Some time ago, I called an old friend that we had not seen or heard from for some time. "How are you doing?" I asked. There was a moment of silence. Then he went on to tell me how bad things were. He had been out of work for some time and the door seemed to shut on every job for which he applied. He mentioned that one of the positions was a job he had believed was the one that was "right" for him. He had gone into the interview full of faith, absolutely convinced it was his. Yet the door had been slammed firmly in his face. He felt God was sadistically toying with him, getting his hopes up, only to shatter them later. A wall had come up between him and the Lord. He was depressed and overwhelmed by how hopeless things looked. In fact, he had become a prisoner of hopelessness and despair. His faith level was very low, and he was locked into a pattern of trying to make things happen for himself rather than seeking the Lord for His counsel, direction and words of life. How had this precious man of God arrived at this point? From what he shared with me, I was able to identify a number of lies that he was believing and acting on, places where he was in agreement with the prince of darkness. These lies had opened a door for the enemy to wreak havoc and destruction in his life, killing his faith, stealing his joy and destroying his hope.

The kinds of lies we believe

There are three primary categories of lies or "ungodly beliefs" that Christians believe. They comprise lies about God, about other people, and about ourselves. All contradict God's Word, nature, character or purposes in some way and are cunningly calculated to sound plausible and right, all the while insidiously releasing the corrupting power of Satan's destruction in our lives. In our years of pastoral and counseling ministry, we have not come across a single Christian who was completely free of ungodly beliefs. Most of us have fallen for a fair number of the enemy's lies. He has been deceiving people for a long time, however, so he is very good at it! He knows just how to twist things in order to ensnare us in his web of deceit.

Lies which we often believe about *ourselves* include some variation of the following:

- I don't belong. I will always be on the outside or left out.
- I am unworthy of God's love or I am unlovable.
- I should have been a boy (or girl). Then my parents would love me more.
- Everything I try goes wrong. I am doomed to failure.
- I am a bad person. If you knew the real me you would reject me.
- This is my life. I am responsible to protect it, provide for it, and get rid of the sin in it.
- My value is in what I can do or achieve.
- There is something wrong with me.

Common lies about *other people* that we often embrace include some of these:

- Other people just want to control me.
- Others don't really like me; they just put up with me.

- Others don't care about me. There is no one to stand with me or support me. I am on my own.
- Authority figures are not trustworthy; they will humiliate or take advantage of me if I allow them to do so.
- What others think of me determines my value.
- No one appreciates me for who I really am.
- Unlike me, other people have it all together.

The following are some of the lies we frequently believe in our hearts about God, irrespective of our theology:

- God is not trustworthy. I cannot depend on Him. He will drop the ball if I really let go of . . . . . . and give it to Him.
- God does not love me as much as He loves everyone else.
- God is waiting for me to make a mistake so He can punish me.
- The way to please God is to devote myself to working for Him.
- God does not love me the way I am. I must be different to receive His love, care or attention.
- God is distant and hard to reach.
- God enjoys watching me suffer.
- God is not interested in the details of my life. He is busy with all the other people He has to watch over.

Exchanging the lies for truth

Identifying the lies that are impacting our lives is only the first step, however, in walking in truth and stepping more fully into our godly inheritance. There is a need to bring our thoughts into captivity to the obedience of Christ (2 Corinthians 10:5), to allow the *exchange* of lies for truth to take place. We can then identify further steps in this exchange process as we allow Jesus the Truth to permeate our lives more completely.

Once we see the lie, it is necessary to take it to the Lord and confess our sin (1 John 1:9). Believing the enemy's lies and coming into covenant with him is sin, and any unconfessed sin stands as a barrier between us and the Lord. We must also forgive ourselves for believing the lie and forgive the people who have reinforced the lie in our lives. For example, if we have believed we were stupid and worthless, there is a need to forgive those who treated us as if we were stupid or worthless or who called us those things. Any unforgiveness in our hearts will stand as a barrier to the release of God's redeeming power in our lives.

Finally, it is imperative that we renounce the lie and reject it as false. I am reminded of something we used to say as children when we recognized that another child was telling a lie. We would instantly shout, "Liar, liar, pants on fire!" As adults, we need to catch the devil in his lies more frequently and instantly brand him for the liar that he is! One big mistake people often make, though, is in trying to receive God's truth and come into agreement with Him *before* they have broken their agreement with the enemy and his lies. We cannot put something new in place if we are still hanging onto the old! As we submit our hearts and minds to the Lord, seeking to exchange the lies for God's truth, it is also important that we pray for revelation. Ask the Holy Spirit to breathe upon the truth and make it living and active in your life. There is a tremendous difference in merely reading words on a page in the Bible and the Lord illuminating those same words and speaking them to our hearts. Life-impacting truth may begin as information (head knowledge). However, it must move from our heads to our hearts and become revelation to us if it is to transform our lives.

The way we think can be a habit as much as smoking, biting our fingernails or scratching our heads when we are puzzled. It often takes 30 days or more to break a habit, that is, to unlearn one mode of behavior and learn another. Therefore, it is important to reinforce the new way of thinking in our devotional time for at least a month after we receive God's truth. We may accomplish this by declaring His truth over ourselves as Christ's ambassadors. Revelation 12:11 reveals how the end-time saints will overcome the enemy. It will be by the blood of the Lamb *and the word of their testimony*. When we declare what the Creator has said about who we are, who He is, and His plan and eternal purposes, His creative power is released to bring about the very things which He has spoken. When we come into agreement with Him here on earth, it *shall* be done (Matthew 18:19).

Establishing the truth in our lives

The Lord will test the truth we have received to establish it firmly in our lives. This is part of the refining process through which He takes each of us.

▶ *The heat and pressure of the test strengthens His truth within us like steel is strengthened in the furnace. It then becomes a part of who we are!*

He intends that we not only wear the belt of truth, part of the spiritual armor He has provided (Ephesians 6:14), but that we manifest Jesus the Truth (2 Corinthians 4:10–11) in a greater way as we go about our daily lives at home, at work, in the grocery store, and on the highway. It is all part of Christ, the *Living* Word, becoming our life.

Earlier in this chapter, I shared about my struggles with completely trusting God, especially in the area of finances and provision. Through the years, the more the truth of His faithfulness has been worked into my life, the more the Lord has tested it. Almost all of our married life we have been self-employed or dependent upon commissions or tips for income. Rarely, have we had a salary or regular paycheck. Time after time, our financial situation looked bleak and we often felt as though we were moving from one test to another in this area with little relief. Little did we know that the Lord was hardening this truth within us to prepare us for what was further on ahead.

After sixteen years of this refining process, the Lord sent us on the mission field. I thought my understanding of God's faithfulness to provide for us was strong and secure until this happened! Because of government regulations, we could not legally work in England, so our income had to be in the form of gifts and donations from people in the States. This circumstance required that we move to a new level of revelation regarding God's faithfulness and care for us. Then the Lord began to speak to us about purchasing a house in that country as a means to breaking through some spiritual barriers there. We were, of course, living hand to mouth and had no money to embark upon such a step. A stretch! About a year after the purchase and the subsequent breakthrough, He began to speak to us about purchasing a commercial building for the ministry. An even bigger stretch! We had never bought a commercial building before. Our church in the States had leased premises. Now the Lord was telling us to buy commercial property in a foreign country and, again, we had no resources at all with which to work! When we found the building the Lord said was His choice, we discovered as we explored financing options that we would need a down payment or deposit of £17,000, the equivalent of about $25,000 at the time. I dreaded every meeting with the bank manager because I knew we didn't have a penny! I also knew, however, that this was the Lord's idea, the building He had picked, and that what we were doing was in simple obedience to His directives. I knew that He is a creative God, not limited by what we have or what we can see. He was just working this truth deeper into our lives!

In the end, the building appraised for £30,000 more than the purchase price and the bank dropped the required down payment to only a few thousand pounds. Not only did the funds arrive before the critical day, but there was an abundance to re-carpet, as well as buy some furnishings and needed equipment. Once we had the loan, the concern then arose in my mind that we, perhaps, could not afford the payments. After all, the ministry was giving much more than it was receiving! However, the Lord brought continual reassurance that this was His plan and He would see it through. He challenged us to be willing to risk and step out of the boat as Peter did in obedience to His call. He also challenged us to believe in Him rather than the in lies of the enemy which were fostering fear and worry in our hearts. In the end, there was never a late payment on the mortgage. The money was always there when we needed it. What a testimony of God's faithfulness! This experience established even more securely in my own heart the truth about His care and concern for me, His faithfulness to live up to His Word, and His ability to triumph over the impossible!

What lies are part of your internal belief system? Where has the enemy got an open door in your life through your agreement with him? How is the Lord testing and establishing His truth in your life at this time? I pray that you will consider these questions and allow the Lord to usher you into a new level of repentance or change in thinking. Exchanging the lies for God's truth is another key to apprehending the riches of His kingdom and walking in the fullness of our godly inheritance!

Prayer

Father, I recognize that many of my thoughts and attitudes are not in agreement with Your Word, nature, character, will or purposes for me. I accept that I am holding many ungodly beliefs that have been shaped by factors that have influenced my life outside of Your grace. In fact, they are lies of the enemy that are holding me captive and creating an open door for him to steal, kill and destroy in my life. Lord, today I choose to break any covenant I have unwittingly made with the enemy through my agreement with his lies. I confess it as sin and receive Your forgiveness. I also forgive myself and anyone who has reinforced these lies in my life, in any way. I renounce each lie and break the power of the lie over me as I apply the blood of Jesus to my mind and thoughts. I choose today to come into agreement with You, Lord. For each lie I have been believing about You, others or myself, I receive Your truth into my heart and life today. I invite You to renew my mind. Let Your words be life to my soul. Holy Spirit, I invite you to breathe upon the truth and illuminate it to my heart. Let it become revelation in me that transforms my life. May Jesus the Truth become manifest in my life in a greater way. Amen.

Note

1. Chester and Betsy Kylstra, *Restoring the Foundations*, 2nd edn, paperback (Proclaiming His Word Publishing, Santa Rosa Beach, FL, 2001), p. 157.

Chapter 12

Will the Real Me Please Stand Up!

For the first twenty years of my walk with the Lord, I believed a huge number of lies about myself. I did not recognize them as lies, however. I thought they were the truth! I believed that I was fat, ugly, defiled, inadequate, unable to communicate, undeserving, damaged, uncared for, alone, worthless and in need of attention. Believing all those lies made me so insecure! Of course, no one knew I believed these things about myself because outwardly I was careful to put up a good front. Also, I was trying very hard to prove myself wrong! I worked overtime to look competent, useful, efficient, successful and outgoing so that no one would see the depths of the inner insecurity and anxiety that I carried. I became the quintessential type-A personality, an overachiever driven to perform and prove my value to the world. However, by the time I was in my mid to late thirties, the stress of pushing so hard and covering up so much was beginning to severely affect me. That is when the Lord began to show me the childhood experiences that had led me to believe so many lies about myself. He exposed what was behind the incredible pain I had felt as a young adult, a pain so intense that I had tried to escape it by burying myself in promiscuity and binge drinking. Step by step, He revealed what was at the root of my misery and insecurity.

The childhood traumas I experienced had opened a door for shame to become firmly rooted in my life. The voice of shame was insistent, telling me that there was something wrong with me, and that I wasn't as good as everyone else. Others might deserve God's blessing in their lives but I did not. I was irreparably damaged, a broken doll that could never be put right

127

again. Bad things would always happen to me. Nothing good would ever last because no one really cared for me, not even God. I felt I was always one step away from losing my hold on life, locked into a vicious cycle – overwhelmed by shame, driven by fear, and working hard to control everything so the shame and the fear would not show. As my life began to unravel and I could see clearly for the first time some of the issues with which I was struggling, Dave and I were introduced to some Spirit-led Christian counselors. Through the relationship with them and the counseling received through their ministry, the childhood traumas were finally put to rest and a great deal of healing was realized in my life. In this process, which has continued through the years, He has set me free from much of the shame that plagued me during the first half of my lifetime. Like everyone, I continue to grow in healing and freedom, but I have changed so much that I am like a different person. I read newspaper accounts sometimes about different celebrities "battling their inner demons". I think to myself, "I used to be like that!" and my heart is filled with gratitude towards the Lord. Because of His faithfulness to put a finger on the shame in my life, battling the inner demons is a thing of the past!

The impact of shame

Shame is the least recognized of the harmful baggage that we carry with us into the kingdom of God. Yet, ironically, I believe it is the baggage that wields the most destructive power in the Body of Christ, second only to unforgiveness! I do not believe we have counseled a single person over the past decade that has not been held captive by shame to some degree or another.

▶ *Shame hinders millions of God's people around the world from stepping into the fullness of the inheritance He purchased for them by the blood of His Son.*

It is shame that makes us feel like God's stepchildren. Because of shame, we do not feel that we really belong in God's family or that we are equal members of His Body. Consequently, we do not reach out to apprehend the inheritance that He sacrificed so much to purchase for us.

As mentioned in our chapter on authority, Jesus said, *"the kingdom of heaven suffers violence and the violent take it by force"* (Matthew 11:12). God's kingdom does not automatically come in our lives. We must go after it, actively pursue it, forcefully press through all the obstacles to grab hold of it. We cannot be timid! When we are bound by shame, however, we do not make the effort because deep down in our hearts we do not believe it is meant for *us*. We reject the fullness and glorious magnitude of the free gift of salvation purchased by Jesus for us at the cross because we feel so worthless.

▶ *Shame keeps us crawling with difficulty through life, accepting the curses of the enemy as our inheritance rather than the blessing of God.*

Shame keeps us living at a spiritual standard that is far below poverty level. We do not actively pursue His kingdom because we do not believe we are capable of reaching it. Shame breeds passivity. We are sure we will fail anyway, so why try?

Shame fuels self-rejection, self-condemnation and self-hate. It also incites a lack of forgiving towards ourselves for being so despicable. Those bound by shame are often angry people. They are angry with themselves, but this anger often spills out onto others like a river that has burst its banks. Sometimes the anger is repressed and manifests itself in the person's life as depression. Those bound by shame often struggle mightily with depression.

Shame locks us into an ungodly cycle of oppression. Because we are convinced that there is something wrong with us, it opens the door for fear to gain a foothold in our lives. What if others find out how worthless, disqualified, or disgusting we really are? They will surely reject or abandon us! We will not hold their respect. We might even be embarrassed or ridiculed. This fear then opens another door for the enemy in the area of control. Because of the fear of what others will think, we begin to control how much of ourselves they actually see. We control our circumstances, always operating in our comfort zone and in the area of our strengths so that our weaknesses won't show. This cycle of oppression sucks the life out of us. The shame batters us. The fear ravages us. And the control takes all our energy. We are so busy "maintaining" that we have little energy left to pursue the kingdom of God!

Finally, shame hinders us from finding out who we really are in Christ. Because the person God created us to be has been buried under layers of shame, fear and control for so long, we have not got a clue as to who we really are! That makes it very easy for us to listen to the voice of shame.

It is important to realize that shame is not so much an emotional or psychological issue as a *spiritual* one. Because it is a spiritual issue, it must be dealt with in a spiritual way. This is why secular psychology cannot effectively help people get free from shame and walk in their true identity. The sense of shame is fueled by the accuser of the brethren that stands, before God, to accuse His people day and night (Revelation 12:10). It is our accusing adversary, Satan, who desires to keep us beaten down, living below our privileges in Christ, and believing that we don't deserve God's best. He is the one who comes to kill, steal and destroy in our lives. He wants us to believe that we are no good, useless and good for nothing. When we believe his lies, we become paralyzed and our greatest fears are realized as that paralysis infiltrates every part of our lives.

Shame brings a false concept of who we are

I once had a friend who would retort when people treated her with less than respect, "What do I look like? Chopped liver?" She was joking, but for those of us bound by shame it is no laughing matter. The devil has convinced us that we *are* chopped liver! That is what we *feel* like, so it *must* be true. The enemy erects in us an entire identity that is false, based on lies that we believe about ourselves. We fall for these lies hook, line and sinker! This identity is false because it is not based on what God says about us, or who God created us to be in His image. If we want to see what our true identity is, all we have to do is look at God Himself.

In enticing us to believe his lies, the enemy will often try to confuse what *we have done* with who we are. It is important to distinguish between the two because there is forgiveness and cleansing available from the Lord for what we have done. There is a remedy for our guilt in the blood of Jesus. If, however, the devil can confuse the issue and convince us that what we have done affects who we are, then it seems hopeless doesn't it? We believe we cannot change who we are. For the same reason, the enemy will also try to confuse our experiences, or *what has been done to us*, with who we are. If we have experienced rejection in the past, he will try to convince us that this is part of our identity – that we are a rejected person whose destiny is more rejection. This is a lie! It is not who God created us to be. It is not His plan and purpose for us. If we buy into the lie, we will feel that all is hopeless, and we will expect more rejection. This expectation will, in turn, cause us to behave differently and bring about the very rejection we were sure was going to happen. Our experience then reinforces the lie that rejection is part of who are and we continue to spiral downwards, overwhelmed by more and more and rejection. Do you see how the devil's cycle of oppression works to subtly rob us of the security and blessing found in our true identity?

I see this robbery blatantly occurring in the lives of those living gay and lesbian lifestyles. The enemy has promulgated a horrendous lie, which the world system has bought into and holds up as "fact". Many Christians have fallen for this deception as well. It is the lie that people are *born* gay or bisexual and that their sexual proclivity is sealed because *this is who they are*. The devil has very aptly confused what people have done with who they are. We have ministered to many people struggling with some form of homosexuality through the years. Without exception, each came to the conclusion that they *must be* gay or lesbian because of an experience or series of experiences at some point in their life, usually as a child or young teenager. Once they accepted the lie and received this false identity, it opened a wider demonic door, allowing even more deception to flood into their lives. Before long, they had become locked into such a cycle of oppression that they had no hope left of escaping. Many precious people *resign* themselves to a gay, lesbian or bisexual lifestyle because they are convinced that this is their identity, the card fate has dealt them, and they must make the best of it. Yet their decision is based on a lie that enables the enemy to continue to kill, steal and destroy in their lives. It is so tragic!

The origin of shame

Looking in the Scriptures, the first appearance of shame occurs in the third chapter of Genesis. At the end of Genesis 2, Adam and Eve are described as naked and *unashamed*. Shame then appears for the first time in Genesis 3, just after the fall of man into sin.

▶ *Note that the emergence of sin into the world brought shame!*

After the fall, the Lord walked through garden looking for the man and woman. He called out to them, *"Where are you, Adam?"* The couple had retreated behind the bushes, however, aware of their nakedness for the first time. Adam replied to the Lord, *"I was afraid because I was naked; and I hid myself"* (Genesis 3:10). They were overcome with shame and fearful of exposure. This is why they were hiding from God. This is why we hide from God as well! When they finally came out from behind the bushes, they tried to cover up their shame with fig leaves. The fig leaves were Adam and Eve's attempt to deal with the shame by human effort.

▶ *We use all sorts of modern fig leaves to cover up our shame.*

I made good grades, won awards, achieved a great deal of recognition, was even listed in *Who's Who* – all things to cover my nakedness and keep my shame from being exposed! Other people use passivity, nonchalance or emotional withdrawal as fig leaves to cover their shame. Most of us also wear masks to cover our shame and hide ourselves from one another. These masks are the faces we put on to make ourselves more acceptable to other people. They look nice but they are fake! Like artificial flowers, they bear only a superficial resemblance to our true identity. There is a fragrance of life that is missing. We all have our personal fig leaves – coping mechanisms that we think work for us. Adam and Eve's fig leaves were not an effective or permanent remedy for their shame, and neither are ours. Human effort is never enough to satisfy or resolve a spiritual issue! Most of us find that the fig leaves we've been using begin to wear thin by the time we get to middle age. Mid-life can be a time of increased insecurity and anxiety if we have not discovered the permanent remedy for shame that the Lord provides.

God promises freedom from shame

Joel 2 is one place where we observe in the Scriptures that shame and God's kingdom appear to be mutually exclusive! The Lord seems quite adamant that He does not want His people afflicted with shame,

> *"You shall eat in plenty and be satisfied,*
> *And praise the name of the* LORD *your God,*
> *Who has dealt wondrously with you;*
> *And **My people shall never be put to shame.***
> *Then you shall know that I am in the midst of Israel:*
> *I am the* LORD *your God*
> *And there is no other.*
> ***My people shall never be put to shame.***"   (Joel 2:26–27)

Not only does the Lord stand against the shame in our lives, but He promises a double portion of the very opposite for His people! He promises honor instead of shame! Isaiah 61 tells us,

> ***"Instead of your shame you shall have double honor,***
> *And instead of confusion they shall rejoice in their portion.*
> *Therefore in their land they shall possess double;*
> *Everlasting joy shall be theirs."*   (Isaiah 61:7)

One day the Lord also fastened my gaze upon Zephaniah 3:19, which reads in the NIV,

> *"At that time I will deal*
>   *with all who oppressed you;*
> *I will rescue the lame*
>   *and gather those who have been scattered.*
> ***I will give them praise and honor***
>   ***in every land where they were put to shame."***

He spoke something into my heart from this verse concerning the shame I had carried. He told me that in every area or land in my life where shame had ruled, that there was a New Covenant appointment to praise and honor! In those places of weakness, the places where I had carried shame for so long, He would now be made strong in my life. It is true! Many years later, those areas of shame in my life now stand as a testimony of God's faithfulness. The areas of my life that were so broken and so devastated by trauma are now the very areas out of which I minister God's love and compassion to the lost and the hurting. The areas of my life that were filled with embarrassment and fear are also the very ones through which He now works. For example, I was so timid at one time that I could not pray out loud in front of another person, even my own husband. I felt incapacitated, useless and ashamed of my inability to communicate. Now I can stand before hundreds of people and pray with confidence that the Anointed One is praying through me. This is just one example of how God has restored the shameful places of my life to bring glory and honor to Him!

The permanent remedy for shame

God's remedy for shame in the book of Genesis was a bit different from Adam and Eve's. Instead of fragile fig leaves, He covered them with skins made from animals (Genesis 3:21). It was necessary for the animals to be killed in order for their skins to be used by God as a covering for fallen man. This act was a foreshadowing of the sacrifice Jesus would make of His own life to cover and free us from sin and shame. However, the animal skins were still not a permanent solution. Jesus gave us a permanent remedy for shame!

▶ *This permanent remedy for shame is found only in Him as we appropriate the blood of Jesus for ourselves and allow Him to be Lord over every part of our lives.*

Remember that with sin, came shame. Where we have unconfessed sin in our lives, shame has a right to remain. 2 Corinthians 4:2 speaks of renouncing the hidden things of shame and becoming a "manifestation" of God's truth. Becoming a manifestation of His truth means *living* the truth – that which is the opposite of feigned or false, therefore in transparent openness and honesty. His permanent remedy for shame offers us the garment of His righteousness, a covering for our shame that can only be obtained through Jesus Christ Himself (Revelation 3:18). The permanent remedy offered by Jesus gives us the right and power to break agreement with the enemy (where we have agreed with his lies), and to take authority over every spirit of shame as we ask the Lord to come in and heal the hurts that opened a door for shame.

Both Romans 9:33 and 1 Peter 2:6 refer to prophetic passages in the book of Isaiah, and exalt Jesus as the cornerstone in Zion who removes and keeps from shame those who put their faith in Him. *He* is the answer to shame! The answer is not in self-esteem programs or positive thinking. Freedom from shame is found only in Him and in His sacrificial death that provided atonement for sin and all the accompanying shame.

Romans 5:12–18 and 1 Corinthians 15:21–22 reveal that Jesus has nullified and overcome every negative thing that the first man, Adam, did. He brought death. Jesus brought life! In the New Testament, Jesus is also called the *"last Adam"* (1 Corinthians 15:45). The first Adam opened the door for sin and its resulting shame to plague humankind. The last Adam shut that door!

As Jesus went to the cross, He *despised* the shame that He carried there as our Redeemer (Hebrews 12:1–2). The Greek word used when this epistle was penned paints a picture of having little or no regard for the shame. It is a picture of renouncing and denouncing the shame, of giving no place to it. We are called to come to the cross daily and walk in the footsteps of Jesus, not only in terms of our willingness to humbly submit our hearts and lives to the Father, but also in terms of walking in the grace and power of God. This can only happen as we, too, "despise" the shame by renouncing it, utterly rejecting it and choosing to give it no place in our lives. As we do so, we will discover that freedom from shame can be a reality for each of God's children, enabling us to step more completely into the glorious inheritance He has provided for us!

Prayer

Father, I am bringing to You all my shame today and laying it at Your feet. I am weary of being bound by this shame, and desire to be free from it. Lord, I also bring to You the fear and the control which have operated in my life along with this shame. It is all sin. Thank You, Jesus, for the new and living way that You have for me to be free from these things! Thank You for Your blood which covers my sin, frees me from all condemnation, and has purchased an inheritance for me. Part of that inheritance is freedom from shame! I reject any predisposition towards shame that I have inherited through my family line and I place the Cross of Jesus Christ between my ancestors and myself today. I receive Your healing, Lord, for any experiences or hurts that opened the door for shame in my life. I choose to forgive all who played a part in those hurts and choose to let go of any unforgiveness, bitterness, resentment, anger, hatred or judgement that I have been holding towards these people.

I also choose today to break all agreement with the enemy about who I am. I renounce all the lies I have believed about myself. I choose today to accept and receive what God says about me and who He says that I am. I reject the false identity the enemy has tried to put on me. Instead, I choose to embrace my true identity – the person God created me to be in His image. I stand against any spirits of shame that have attached themselves to me and I break friendship with them. I choose God's blessing today. I choose the double honor that He promised instead of the shame. I now call forth the "real me", the man or woman of God that He created me to be. Lazarus, come forth! Amen.

Chapter 13

Answering the Cry for Integrity

One of the young teenagers we knew some years ago had the attitude that everything was lawful as long as one does not get caught. There was an arrogance about him, as if he felt that he had some sort of special right or privilege to step over the line. He always had a rationale about why it was okay for him to say or do something hurtful or unethical. He had been raised in a Christian family and been to church all of his life. Where did this attitude come from? It seemed he picked it up from the people around him. While he took it to an extreme, he was acting out what he saw demonstrated in the lives of the people he was observing and imitating. Where they rationalized their lack of integrity and inconsistencies a little bit, he rationalized them a great deal. He merely took things a step farther to their logical conclusion!

Integrity, according to the *Oxford English Dictionary*, is moral uprightness or honesty. *Webster's 1828 American Dictionary of the English Language* adds the idea of purity and freedom from corruption. This dictionary also links the concept of character with integrity. In a biblical sense, we may also define integrity as walking righteously or justly. Righteousness is a part of the nature and character of God. Psalm 11:7 tells us,

> *"For the LORD is righteous,*
> *He loves righteousness;*
> *His countenance beholds the upright."*

Psalm 45:6 reveals that His kingdom's scepter is characterized by righteousness.

▶ *I believe that choosing to walk righteously is a prerequisite for seeing God's kingdom come into our lives in the fullness that He intends.*

137

Proverbs 2:20–21 speaks of keeping to the paths of righteousness,

> *"So you may walk in the way of goodness,*
> *And keep to the paths of righteousness.*
> *For the upright will dwell in the land,*
> *And the blameless will remain in it."*

Of what land does the author of Proverbs speak? He speaks of the promised land, the land of inheritance! For the Israelites it was a physical place. For us it is a spiritual place. However, uprightness or integrity is still required in order to live and walk in that place! In fact, the Word says the kingdom of God *is* righteousness (Romans 14:17). To *live* in righteousness suggests an immersion into it, with righteousness directing our every thought, our every word and every action we take.

Warren Wiersbe wrote in 1988, "We are facing an integrity crisis. Not only is the conduct of the church in question, but so is the very character of the church." He was writing at time when the Body of Christ was being shaken by scandals involving high profile leaders. However, Wiersbe went on to caution his readers, "The integrity crisis involves the whole church."[1] Fifteen years later, I do not believe this crisis of integrity has been resolved. We are still in the midst of an integrity crisis! It goes much deeper than the excesses of the televangelists, adulterous relationships, misappropriating funds, or of the things that we have come to associate with lack of integrity in the Church. I believe the rot is deeper and more widespread, at the very core of our beings, and revealed in our everyday attitudes and actions. Integrity is really about godly character and how much of that character is manifest in our lives. Perhaps we should describe the current state of affairs as a "character crisis". Our lack of integrity is actually the fruit of our failure to allow God to develop His character in us.

The need for integrity in the everyday things

▶ *Evidence of a character void can be seen in our everyday lives.*

When I was working my way through college as a waitress, I saw it in the restaurants where I worked. No one that I worked with would want to be put on the schedule for Sundays. Why? It was not because they wanted to go to church! It was because they were run ragged, yet only made half their usual income on Sundays. The Christians would come in after church and fill the restaurant to overflowing, then be imperious and demanding, leaving very little in the way of a tip. Because those tips constituted most of their salary as wait staff, my co-workers depended on them to support their families and pay their bills. What made it even sadder, however, was the fact that the worldly people who came in were often much nicer. They treated the wait staff better, they were more polite and understanding when problems arose, and they were generally much more generous in their giving! This illustrates to me a crisis of character among Christians. It is the kind of everyday situation where real character is revealed. For some, we will be the only expression of Jesus they will ever know. What are we demonstrating?

I see many people driving around with the fish sign on the back of their car to show the world they are Christians. Often they are speeding significantly above the posted speed limit. What does this show the world about their character? Are we really a witness of God's character and integrity when we flout the laws of the land, rationalizing that they don't apply to us because we are in a hurry? Some of my American Christian friends have radar detectors in their vehicles. They not only speed, they plan to do it and make provision for how they can speed without suffering any consequences. So often, we just do what everyone else does, think the way the world thinks, and never give it a second thought. We don't even realize the shortage of integrity that is revealed.

Gossip is another area where I believe Christians exhibit a lack of integrity every day. Most of us would be horrified by the thought of an adulterous relationship, but we think nothing of spreading gossip. Sin is sin, however. There really isn't good sin and bad sin. In God's eyes, it is just as loathsome. The book of Proverbs cautions about gossip at least five times. There are numerous New Testament passages about gossip. One, Romans 1:29, equates gossip with wickedness, evil, greed and depravity. Gossip can be spread under the guise of sharing prayer requests. I know of a pastor who violated the confidentiality of the counseling relationship to share with others in the church what he had been told in counseling by an individual. He rationalized this lack of integrity by saying he was only asking people to pray for this individual. His gossip resulted in further gossip, and before long, it was all over town. It is so easy for *any of us* to slide into gossip before we know it. However, I believe we need to be forthright in our assessment that gossip demonstrates a lack of integrity. A commitment to guard our tongues and our hearts from gossip brings us a step closer to the manifestation of God's kingdom and His righteousness in our lives.

Financial integrity

▶ *I have noticed that with Christians, much of our lack of integrity involves either our mouths or our money!*

Finances or business dealings are another area where our lack of character or integrity shows up in the everyday things. When Dave was working in construction, the only job for which he was never paid was one he did for a Christian. The man kept saying he didn't have the money, until Dave finally gave up trying to collect. I have a friend in Texas who has worked for a succession of Christian bosses. Almost every one of them has taken advantage of her in some way, usually financially. The last one owed her $700 for two weeks work. By the time I came to visit her last year, she was in desperate financial straits. She had been trying to get her final check from this woman for a quite some time, but the woman continued to avoid her or put her off. She had finally tracked the woman down and gotten her permission to come and pick up the check at her house. We drove over and picked up the check, which was in a sealed envelope. As we drove away, my friend said, "Dee, you open it. I'm scared to even look. I'm afraid she didn't make the check for the full amount." I opened the envelope and the check was for less than $200.

Here is an interesting story. We received an email once from a man who had gotten our name and address off another ministry's mailing list. This total stranger explained in a bulk email sent out that he and his wife wanted to buy a house. They needed something like $30,000 for a down payment on the house of their dreams. He further explained that God had told him that all of us strangers on this mailing list were to help him buy his house by giving him the down payment. He was writing to let us know what God had said and to give us the golden opportunity to partner with God in this endeavor. I have to confess that my first thought was, "Get a life, Buddy!" It was only as I thought about it for a while that I began to grieve over how low we have fallen in the area of financial integrity.

A similar thing happened recently. We received *another* generic email from *another* total stranger who took our name and address off someone else's mailing list. It was from a man in an African country writing to say that he, a former government official, had been gloriously converted from Islam to Christianity. Unfortunately, when he was still a government official he had stolen the equivalent of thousands of dollars from the government. Now, he explained, the Lord was telling him to give it all (the *stolen* money) to a deserving Christian ministry as restitution for his dark deed. Wonderfully, he had picked ours! He went on to explain that he needed details of where the cash could be delivered. As an aside at the end of the letter, he mentioned that he and his whole family would like to travel to our location to personally meet us once we received the money. Then he made a few more statements that, reading between the lines, indicated they were really fleeing prosecution and looking for some suckers who would be so blinded by greed that they wouldn't question the honesty, ethics or legalities of this transaction. The sad thing is that someone on the mailing list probably responded.

Christians in the pews are certainly not the only ones exhibiting lack of integrity concerning money. Through the years I have heard some of the sad stories told by evangelists and itinerant ministers who had offerings taken up for them, but then found out later that they had been given only a portion of the offering. The pastor would tell the congregation that this was a love offering specifically for this individual to bless them and their ministry, but then they would keep back part of the money for church expenses. The traveling ministers usually found out later quite by accident. We experienced something similar as missionaries when a lovely lady in a local fellowship asked us if we had been getting the monthly contribution she had been giving to her pastor to send us. We had not. He had been taking her money and using it for other things. Either he rationalized that we would never know or that other things were more important. Either way, this is lack of integrity folks!

Living up to our word

Another place where I see a lack of integrity among Christians is in not honoring our word. As Christians, our word should mean more than the word of an unsaved person who has not had the benefit of the blood of Jesus working in his life to set him free from the power of sin! Yet, Christians can be the flakiest people on earth. My husband, Dave, calls these people "cereal Christians" – fruits, nuts and flakes. It wouldn't be so bad if there weren't so many Christians like this. It is as if we have fallen into the trap of being Christians in name only, or what a dear friend of mine calls "armchair Christians". Armchair Christians have a deep and abiding awareness of God's grace, but lack the equal and opposite awareness of His holiness and righteousness. Somehow their faith has never worked its way deep enough into their heart to impact their life and character! They are those who hear the Word over and over again, but never become "doers" of it (James 1:22).

Our children, being the offspring of pastors and missionaries, have seen a great deal of this "flakiness", both in the United States and in other countries. Flakiness and lack of integrity are not limited to any specific culture! Their commentary is one that should make us take notice. Not too long ago, we were preparing to leave them in our house to finish university in one country, while we answered God's call to move elsewhere. However, they needed to get a housemate in order to be able to afford the rent. As we were discussing the options, my daughter said, "Mom, I think we would rather get a housemate who is clean and doesn't smoke, but who is not a Christian." My son surprisingly agreed. Puzzled, I asked them why. My daughter responded, "Because a lot of times non-Christians are easier to deal with." I asked her what she meant by this and she continued, "Well, it's just that Christians often try to weasel out of responsibility by appealing to your requirement to forgive them. We don't want the hassle." It was an insightful comment from a twenty-one year old, but a sad commentary on the Church in relation to our level of character and integrity.

Does the end really justify the means?

Another area where a lack of integrity shows frequently is in the common reasoning that "the end justifies the means". We think that because our motives are right, that we want to help people or do something big for God, it means it is all right to use methods that are a controlling, manipulative or deceptive. Leaders rationalize that it is all right to manipulate with guilt, or pressure people into giving, because it is for a good cause or because it is "helping people" learn to walk in God's principles of giving. Or they think it is fine to use people like slaves to build their ministry because the bigger their ministry, the more people they can touch with God's life and power. However, leaders are not the only Christians who fall prey to the deception that the end justifies the means. How often are *any* of us tempted to cut corners on a job, fudge things on our taxes or misrepresent things only slightly because of what is to be gained? How often do we succumb to these temptations?

How often do we step over the line of integrity just a little because we have convinced ourselves it will be for someone else's benefit? Here is a good example. We recently got an email from a woman who had taken our name off a mutual friend's email to her. Because the mutual friend had not sent a blind carbon copy of his email to us and the rest of his friends, all of our email addresses were on the correspondence. This woman, who is in some sort of Christian multi-level marketing scheme, then sent a personal promotional email to all of us, playing upon the relationship with the mutual friend. Of course, the mutual friend knew nothing about this until much later! I am sure that this woman had convinced herself that her lack of integrity was balanced out by the good she was doing us. After all, she was giving us the opportunity to make lots of extra money, as well as expand her own business. In short, she had fallen prey to the deception that the end justifies the means!

How godly character is developed

God's plan is to build character in us – *His* character. My carnal nature is rebellious and driven by the lust of the eyes, the lust of flesh and the pride of life. My carnal nature is also self–seeking, greedy, lazy and primarily concerned with what I want. It desires to look out for "number one" – me! I suspect that your carnal nature is much like mine! Our attitudes, motives and desires do not change the moment we open our hearts to Jesus, however. Though we can legally stand before God as righteous, because our sin is covered by the blood of Jesus (2 Corinthians 5:21; Philippians 3:9), that judicial righteousness has often not had the chance to work itself down into the fibre of our lives. This happens only as we *submit* our hearts and wills to the processes of God as He works in us *"to will and do of His good pleasure"* (Philippians 2:13) and to restore us back to His image. It is only as we *cooperate* with the Lord in His refining work in our lives (Malachi 3:2–4), that His righteousness becomes ours, changing who we are and the way we live. It is the Lord's responsibility to change us but we have the responsibility to work with Him!

We make a huge mistake in comparing ourselves to the world. We often think that as long as we are a notch above the world, we are doing well! However, as the moral integrity of the world has plummeted over the past 40 years or so, the moral uprightness of the Church has plummeted right along with it! It is not with the world that we should be comparing ourselves. It is with the Lord. We should not be asking ourselves, "Am I more upright than the people around me?" We should be asking ourselves, "How close am I to God's standard of holiness and justice? How much of His character and nature am I exhibiting?" The "WWJD" wristbands popular among young people to remind them to ask, "What would Jesus do?", are a step towards highlighting the importance of character and integrity. However, knowing that character and integrity is important is one thing. Understanding *how* God's character and integrity is developed in us is quite another!

▶ *It takes continued surrender over time for God to build His character and nature in us.*

It means coming to Gethsemane *over and over again*, in one situation after another, making the choice "not my will but Yours be done". That means trusting Him and committing ourselves to do things His way, even when we are scared to death of what it might cost us. As Psalm 37 says,

"Commit your way to the LORD,
Trust also in Him,
And He shall bring it to pass.
He shall bring forth your righteousness as the light,
And your justice as the noonday."   (Psalm 37:5–6)

Godly character is built in us as we go through trials and difficult situations with a yielded heart and the right attitude. The book of Hebrews tells us that Jesus learned obedience through the things that He suffered (Hebrews 5:8). Romans 6:13–16 reveals that obedience to God leads to righteousness being worked out in our lives. Receiving the Lord's correction also works righteousness into our lives (Hebrews 12:11). Integrity or righteousness is something that must be pursued or sought after (1 Timothy 6:11; 2 Timothy 2:22). It doesn't just happen automatically! Further, we must apply it to our lives, or "put it on". Psalm 132:9 admonishes, *"Let your priests be clothed with righteousness."* Remember that New Testament saints stand as a royal priesthood before God. The Apostle Paul echoes the psalmist in Ephesians 4:24 by stressing how needful it is *"that you put on the new man which was created according to God, in true righteousness and holiness".* The person we were meant to be all along was created in God's image, that of righteousness and holiness. This is our true identity! We have to "put it on", however, by surrendering our carnal man to death and applying God's Word to our lives!

Finally, the Lord builds His character in us as we determine to press forward in Him through every hindrance and every obstacle. It takes a tenacious attitude like that of the Apostle Paul's. He wrote,

*"Brethren, I do not count myself to have apprehended; but one thing I do, forgetting those things which are behind and reaching forward to those things which are ahead, I **press toward the goal** for the prize of the upward call of God in Christ Jesus."*
        (Philippians 3:13–14)

All hell and every temptation of the flesh will resist us in our decision to press toward that goal and that upward call, walking uprightly and with integrity. But God provides the grace necessary to answer His calling and to walk in it. Sometimes we are waiting to see the grace before we step out to answer the call. However, the grace is released *as* we step out!

Walking the talk

Our motive, message and methods must reflect the character of Christ if we are to be people of integrity. However, we are not left on our own to accomplish it. The Spirit of the Lord will guide us in this endeavor! The Psalmist understood this when he penned the well-known Twenty-third Psalm, *"He leads me in paths of righteousness"* (Psalm 23:3). He will lead us into all truth. He is our Counselor and the One who brings conviction. Granted, it is far easier to listen to the voice of human reason that says things like, "everyone does it", "no one will know", "it's only a little thing" or "it is better not to make waves".

▶   *Righteousness and integrity will only become ours, however, if we respond to the nudge of the Holy Spirit when He brings the conviction that something we are about to do or say is a little "off".*

If we will listen to Him, instead of ignoring Him or pushing Him away, we will find that our lives run more smoothly and are characterized by His peace. Further, we will manifest more and more of the character of Jesus Christ to the people around us!

A woman I know, who stands out brightly as a person of character and integrity, was sharing with me recently the process she went through with the Lord to become the woman she is today. She related that as a young Christian, the Holy Spirit would not let her get away with anything! He would keep bringing back to her mind the things she had said and done that weren't quite right. Because her heart was soft and sensitive to Him, she didn't ignore Him even though, as she admitted, it would have been a very easy thing to do. Often she would be cleaning and going about her daily routine in tears as the Lord was bringing His conviction. She humorously recounted days that she would spend hours scrubbing or vacuuming her house, while inwardly the Lord was scrubbing away on her!

We see in the Scriptures that there is *blessing* in walking righteously and with integrity (Psalm 106:3). Jesus said those who hunger for righteousness will be blessed and filled (Matthew 5:6). Righteousness leads to life (Proverbs 11:19). Proverbs 10:9 reveals that the one who walks in integrity walks securely. We desperately look for security in so many places, but few of us look for it in a life of righteous living! Not only do we *receive* blessing from the Lord when we walk in His righteousness and integrity, but we *are* a blessing. The lives of others are blessed by us as we conduct our relationships justly, in goodness and purity. We are also much more effective in being His witnesses!

I heard the true story not too long ago of an evangelist who was ministering in another country. The details have since blurred in my memory, but the main points of the story are still clear. The bus driver, an unbeliever, recognized the minister when he got on the bus and decided to see if he was genuine. He gave him back too much change and waited to see what would happen. When the minister sat down in his seat, he realized the bus driver had given him back too much money. His companion urged him to keep it, feeling that perhaps it was God's answer to their prayer since they were in desperate need of funds. The minister, however, knew he had to speak with the bus driver and correct the mistake. When he went to the driver, the man's face wreathed in a smile as he shared with the minister that indeed, it had been no mistake, but rather a test! In so many words, the bus driver conveyed to the minister that he had passed the test and for this reason, the bus driver now planned to attend his meetings and would be open to whatever he had to share because it was clear he was "real".

Would you have passed the test? Are you "real" in your Christian walk or are you mostly talk? Could you confidently pray as the psalmist prayed in Psalm 7:8?

> "*Judge me, O* LORD,
> *According to my righteousness,*
> *And according to my integrity within me.*"

These are tough questions that I believe we must each consider carefully if we are to press on to experience the kingdom of God more fully in our lives. Shallow character and lack of integrity will rise up as stumbling blocks if we are not *determined* to allow the Lord to do His refining, conforming, reforming work within us! Will you determine in your heart today, *"But as for me, I will walk in my integrity . . . "* (Psalm 26:11)? As you do, you can trust the Lord to uphold you. The psalmist also wrote,

> *"As for me, You uphold me in my integrity,*
> *And set me before Your face forever."*   (Psalm 41:12)

The Lord promised Solomon that if he walked in the same integrity and uprightness of heart as his father, David, then He would establish him and his authority (1 Kings 9:4). He was reaffirming with Solomon the covenant He had made with David, but it was conditional on Solomon's diligence to set his heart to walk after God. He has made a covenant with us as well (Luke 22:20; Hebrews 12:24). This New Covenant, sealed by the blood of Jesus, is also conditional upon our setting our hearts to *"seek first the kingdom of God and His righteousness"* (Matthew 6:33). Then, He promises, everything that is a part of His kingdom will be *"added to"* us. It is another way of saying that those things that are of His kingdom will be put in our heavenly bank account for us to draw upon as needed. This privilege, however, presupposes our commitment to walk in integrity!

Prayer

Dear Father, I confess to You that I have not sought first Your kingdom and Your righteousness before my own wants and needs. I have allowed myself to be ruled by my carnal man in so many ways. Because of that, I have not walked in the level of righteousness and integrity that You have ordained for me as Your child. I have not unreservedly invited You to build Your character in me, doing the heart work and refining that You have wanted to do in me. Further, I have rationalized my moral failures and areas of my life that have not met Your standard of holiness and justice. I have made excuses for myself and allowed myself to fall prey to the enemy's deception. Lord, I pray that You will forgive me for every time I have missed Your mark in the area of integrity and for every time I have ignored the conviction of Your Holy Spirit when He tried to check me. Thank You for Your forgiveness. I receive it, Lord, and I choose to forgive myself for falling short of your mark. I forgive myself for the rationales and the excuses. As I set my heart today to walk after You fully, and to seek first Your kingdom and Your righteousness, I pray that You will cleanse me as You promised of all unrighteousness (1 John 1:9). I open my heart and my life to You in a deeper way today, Lord, to cleanse, purify, and refine me. I want to be so free of impurities that I shine as a polished jewel in Your hand. I desire, dear Lord, to be so pure that others around me would be able to see Your reflection in my life. Please help me to be obedient and sensitive to Your Spirit, as I commit my entire life to You in a deeper way today. I want to be a person of unquestionable integrity. Amen.

Note

1. Warren Wiersbe, *The Integrity Crisis* (Thomas Nelson Publishers, Nashville, 1988, 1991), pp. 17–18.

Chapter 14

Is It Good or Is It God?

Because I had a number of wonderful brothers and sisters in the Body of Christ to take me under their wing, I learned very early in my walk with the Lord that there is a difference in something being "good" and something being "God". Whenever I have a choice to make, I first differentiate between what *seems* right or good and what is really His leading in the matter. Proverbs 16:25 is a repeat of Proverbs 14:12. Both reveal to us that,

> *"There is a way that **seems right** to a man,*
> *But its end is the way of death."*

I've learned through some agonizing experiences that doing what seems "good" at the time is not terribly productive in terms of learning to live in the kingdom of God. In fact, it has gotten me into big trouble!

▶ *The things I do, the way I do them, and what I say must be God-motivated and God-directed if I am to see His Kingdom come in my life.*

They must also be God-empowered. I learned through the process of trial and error that self-effort and human strength, or our own abilities, will get us into trouble too! Upon many occasions, I was left devastated by a turn of events, crying out to the Lord, "What happened?" or "Why is this not working?" Inevitably, He would show me that I was relying on myself and not on Him.

▶ *We must seek to be enabled, empowered and sustained by Him alone if we are to realize the fullness of His Kingdom in our lives.*

Psalm 20 contrasts the result of relying on the Lord with relying on our own human ability and methods,

> *"Some trust in chariots and some in horses,*
> *but we trust in the name of the LORD our God.*
> *They are brought to their knees and fall,*
> *but we rise up and stand firm."* (Psalm 20:7–8, NIV)

Isaiah and Jeremiah issue a strong warning to God's people about trusting in human effort. Jeremiah 17 says,

> *"Thus says the LORD:*
>
> *'Cursed is the man who trusts in man*
> *And makes flesh his strength,*
> *Whose heart departs from the LORD.*
> *For he shall be like a shrub in the desert,*
> *And shall not see when good comes,*
> *But shall inhabit the parched places in the wilderness,*
> *In a salt land which is not inhabited.'"* (Jeremiah 17:5–6)

Isaiah 31 similarly warns,

> *"Woe to those who go down to Egypt for help,*
> *And rely on horses,*
> *Who trust in chariots because they are many,*
> *And in horsemen because they are very strong,*
> *But who do not look to the Holy One of Israel,*
> *Nor seek the LORD!"* (Isaiah 31:1)

The Apostle Paul called self-sufficiency and self-reliance foolishness! He wrote to the Galatians,

> *"Are you so foolish? After beginning with the Spirit, are you now trying to attain your goal by human effort?"*
> (Galatians 3:3, NIV)

We could sum up by saying the kingdom of God will only be realized in our lives if we are committed to God's plan, God's way, in God's timing. For many, this may sound like plain common sense. But it is a surprising discrepancy that often exists between what we believe we know and how we live our lives! There are a lot of things we know intellectually that never make it down to our hearts to change our attitudes and actions.

Many years ago, I was required to take a physics course that I loathed at university. It was the only course I almost failed! But I learned something in that course which has helped me to understand how spiritual things work (or do *not* work) in us. There was a section in this course on circuits. I learned that a resistor added to a circuit will reduce the flow of current through the circuit. A resistor is made of something that does not conduct well. Using a non-conductor would stop the flow all together. As human beings, I've discovered, we all have a built-in "resistor" called our carnal nature. This natural resistor hinders and sometimes blocks completely the flow of current of God's life and power from our heads to our hearts! Our carnal nature acts as a spiritual inhibitor, causing us to miss God's plan, His way or His timing as we substitute our own. Of course, our own *seem* so good!

Creating Ishmaels

Abraham and Sarah learned the hard way that things that seem good, but are not led of the Lord, will get us in a lot of trouble. They also learned that trying to help God fulfill His promises by human effort creates a lot of unnecessary problems! God had promised Abraham a son (Genesis 15:2–4). When it seemed that the promise was not going to materialize because of Sarah's barrenness, she came up with an idea. Her idea, in essence, was to take matters into their own hands. Though Abraham and Sarah were people of faith, it is clear that both of them had a difficult time believing that God could do the impossible, despite what He had promised (Genesis 17:16–17; 18:10–14). I think that in a moment of weakness, they both yielded to unbelief. Sarah suggested that Abraham go in to her maid, Hagar, and produce a child (Genesis 16:1–4). While this was an accepted custom of the time, it was not God's idea and not His plan. He meant for the child of promise to be Abraham and Sarah's son. He meant for the conception to be a miraculous thing, accomplished by His hand. Abraham, however, agreed with Sarah that going in to Hagar sounded like a good idea. They ended up with Ishmael as a result! The Lord later said He would bless Ishmael, but that His covenant was only with Isaac (Genesis 17:16–21). Isaac was the son of God's promise. Ishmael was the son of human wisdom and effort!

▶ *While God in His grace and mercy may still bless the product of our human effort, His covenant blessing and anointing will not rest on those things.*

The biblical record shows us that Ishmael was a source of constant pain and conflict in the family, so much so that Abraham had to send Hagar and Ishmael away (Genesis 21:8–14). Later, Ishmael became the father of the Arab nations. To this day, the descendants of Ishmael (Arabs) and Isaac (Jews) continue in conflict with one another.

▶ *The Ishmaels we create through our human wisdom and effort will similarly bring conflict into our lives, competing with God's true plan, dividing our attention and our hearts.*

I have been very good at creating Ishmaels through the years! I was accustomed to making things happen in the business world and found it very difficult to change as I grew in my relationship with the Lord. I wanted to plan and direct everything. Even if I could not handle it better than the Lord, I could certainly make it happen faster. He was so slow! Of course, I was doing it in my own strength, using human effort to get the job done rather than relying upon the Lord's timing. It took me many years before it finally dawned on me why I was so tired all the time!

A few years after I recommitted my life to the Lord at age 26, I knew the Lord told me that He would use me in the field of writing. I instantly started to work on a book! Every day while my babies were taking their afternoon naps, I diligently pecked away on my electric typewriter writing the book that was never meant to be. After a year of this, the Lord finally got through to me that He was not in it. He said, "wait" and so I waited – for fifteen years! When He finally initiated a writing project, however, it happened with His divine enabling, His anointing, and His favor.

Another Ishmael developed quite by accident. At one point in our ministry, the Lord was showing us some new things about team ministry and the need to break out of the traditional church mold. In the midst of this new revelation, we were approached by another leader who wanted to join our ministries and work together with us, as a team. We seemed to have the same vision and it appeared to be an opportunity to see the fulfillment of what God was speaking to us about. My husband, Dave, had reservations, but I was quite excited about it all and succeeded in convincing him to give it a chance. Unfortunately, I can be quite enthusiastic and persuasive at times. As we continued to try to work together with this other minister, however, it became more apparent that we had either missed the Lord's perfect plan or His timing. We had jumped into a partnership too quickly, discovering only after a number of months that we had two different visions, even though we used identical words. It became clear that our approach to ministry and even our values were so contrary that there was a great deal of conflict and tension. In the end, huge cracks appeared in the foundation of the work. As we sought the Lord about what to do, He told us to prune the ministry back to the place it was before this man had entered into the picture. We lost a year of progress because of our mistake, but in the end the work flourished and bore much fruit. The Lord is so good and gracious to us, despite our failings and mistakes!

Building new oxcarts

An illustration is found in the Scriptures of another man who tried to fulfill God's purposes in his own human wisdom and effort. This time it was King David. The Lord called David a man after His own heart (1 Samuel 13:14). We use this expression in contemporary society to mean someone who follows after the example of another. However, it could also mean that David was one who sought or pursued God's heart. Certainly, his prayers, his psalms and his life, despite his blunders, seem to suggest this was the case. David was passionate about the presence of God. He sought God and worshiped Him with a whole heart. His priorities were evident in 1 Chronicles 13:12 when he agonized, *"How shall I bring the ark home to me?"* David's passion and wholehearted seeking after the presence of God was a good thing. The Lord used it to restore His presence to His people and to usher in a season of restoration and freedom that fore-shadowed the coming of the Messiah. However, David also made a number of mistakes! Sometimes his passion clouded his judgement and his discernment of God's strategy. One such occasion was His attempt to bring the Ark of the Covenant back to Jerusalem.

The Ark housed the literal presence of God. He manifested His presence between the two cherubim and above the mercy seat that covered it (Exodus 25:22; 1 Samuel 4:4; 2 Samuel 6:2). When the Ark was captured by the Philistines during Saul's reign, it was announced that the visible glory of God had departed from Israel (1 Samuel 4:19–22).

The Philistines had taken the Ark to Ashdod and set it right beside the idol of Dagon in his temple. The presence of God continually caused the idol to fall over on its face, until finally the head and hands broke off completely! The Philistines also experienced a plague that ravaged the entire area. Many scholars think it likely from the description of the plague that it was Bubonic plague. Eventually Ashdod sent the Ark to Gath, where the people there also were struck down with the plague. Gath then sent it to Ekron, where the same thing happened! This account is found in 1 Samuel 5.

Finally the Philistines had had enough! They put the Ark on an oxcart and sent it up the road to Beth Shemesh in Israel. The people of Beth Shemesh rejoiced greatly that the Ark was back, but over fifty thousand were struck down by the Lord for having the presumption to look into it. To look in the Ark, one had to lift the mercy seat out of the way. One had to remove the covering of blood because the blood was applied to the mercy seat. Inside the Ark were the tablets of the law.

► *Looking at the law without God's covering of mercy and the blood of atonement killed them!*

We see the same principle in the New Testament when the Apostle Paul explained, *"the letter kills ... "* (2 Corinthians 3:6).

Out of fear, they called for the men of Kirjath Jearim to come and take the Ark. It then came to rest in Kirjath Jearim at the home of Abinadab for at least another twenty years. During the years that the Ark was with the Philistines and in the house of Abinadab, estimated by some scholars to be as long as one hundred years, worship was continuing in the Tabernacle of Moses. They were going through the motions, saying and doing all the right things, but the presence of God was not there!

1 Chronicles 13:3 implies that during the reign of Saul, no one was concerned or bothered about the fact that they were missing the presence of God. I am sad to report that this same situation exists today. Many Christians are worshiping in places where the presence of God has been gone for a long time! Yet they continue to go through the motions and rituals of worship, either unaware or unconcerned that His anointing is no longer there.

After David became king, the Lord put it on his heart to facilitate the return of His presence to Israel. David, however, did not seek God about the way to go about it. His passion stirred him to impetuously set out to accomplish God's plan in his own way.

▶   *His motives were right, His goal was godly, but the method he used led him into trouble!*

1 Chronicles 13 and 2 Samuel 6 are parallel accounts that detail David's attempt to get the Ark and return the presence of God to Jerusalem. Upon studying these accounts, we can see the mistakes David made. Here are a few of them:

*   He consulted the people instead of the Lord, looking for their affirmation and approval (1 Chronicles 13:3–4). This opened the door for human wisdom and human effort to saturate the plan to retrieve the Ark.

*   Those who went to recover the Ark of the Covenant did not sanctify or consecrate themselves in preparation for being in the presence of a holy God. God had ordained that those who came before Him wash themselves and consecrate themselves before coming into His presence (Exodus 30:19–20; 40:12–13, 31; Leviticus 16:2–4). Jesus illustrated the same principle in John 13:8 when He told Peter, *"if I do not wash you, you have no part with Me."* If we are careless and sloppy in our walk with God, failing to respond when He

brings conviction or when He stirs our hearts to a deeper level of consecration to Him, we may similarly experience failure in our efforts to do godly things.

- They carried the Ark on a new oxcart even though God had ordained that it be carried only on the shoulders of the priests (Numbers 4:5, 6, 15; 7:9; Deuteronomy 10:8; 1 Chronicles 15:2, 15). The Philistines had sent the Ark back on a new cart, which the Israelites broke up and used for firewood for the sacrifice to celebrate the ark's return (1 Samuel 6:14). They probably figured it had worked for the Philistines. Why not do it the same way? They imitated the ways of the religious world around them, instead of doing it God's way. Failure and tragedy were the result.

- Uzza and Ahio were allowed to drive the cart and Uzza to touch the Ark of the Covenant. Uzza means "strength". Ahio means "brotherly". Human strength and human unity, in the form of brotherly love, were driving the new cart representing man's plan and way of doing things. The oxen then stumbled, shaking the Ark. When we try to accomplish things our way, in our own strength, it is a precarious place to be and stumbling is often the result! This happened at the threshing floor, which is the place where the wheat was separated from the chaff.

  ▶ *We all have "threshing floor experiences" in our lives, and it will be a time of stumbling for us if we are operating independently of God.*

Uzza reached out to try to steady the Ark and touched it. This was in contradiction to God's command that no one touch His holy things. He had already warned that they would die if they did (Numbers 4:15). Uzza tried to help God, and in his presumption, had to reap the consequences of his disobedience. In 2 Samuel 6, it uses a Hebrew word that means "irreverence" to describe Uzza's sin.

  ▶ *How often have we dared to put our hands on what God was doing, thinking our effort was needed to help God?*

Uzza's motive was good and honorable but, like David, he didn't handle the situation God's way. It killed him!

We have a tendency to build oxcarts of our own and "drive the cart" with our own human effort. These "vehicles" we create are assembled with human tools, bearing the mark of man's hand upon them. Wood usually symbolizes humanity in the Bible. The fact that the Israelites tried to bring the Ark back on a wooden cart speaks of man's vehicle and plans, man's method or way of doing things. The fact that it was a "new" cart is important. Because it was fresh and exciting to them, they missed the fact that it was not God's way of doing it! The Body of Christ needs discernment of God's plans and strategies. Sometimes we try to employ a "new cart" to carry the presence of God, unaware that "new and different" is not the same as God's plan.

▶ *It can be new and different, and still be the product of human reasoning and effort!*

Some of the movements we have witnessed in the Body of Christ over the past twenty years have been man-made. They have been new carts somebody came up with to carry the presence of God. Recently, I attended a meeting in another city where the speaker made continual reference to a new kind of church they were promoting. It was presented as "this is what everyone is doing now" and we were urged to climb aboard the bandwagon. The implication was that we would be missing God if we didn't. But as I listened, I felt that the people on the bandwagon were making a very common mistake. We often assume that because something is new and different and doesn't look like the old oxcart, it must be God. Many times all we have done is built a new oxcart! Yes, it does look different than the old one. But it is still an oxcart! I pray that we will grow in wisdom and discernment as we learn to abide in Christ, that the oxcarts of our lives will become more and more a thing of the past.

Living like Pharisees

In the New Testament, we read about an entire group of people who missed God by focusing on what seemed "good". They also made the mistake of operating out of human effort and wisdom in their attempt to walk with Him. These men were the religious leaders called Pharisees. Like David, their motives were often pure. They wanted to serve God, honor Him and live lives glorifying to Him. Like David, however, their human reasoning got in the way and their methodology fell far short of God's plan. As a result, they fell into the mire of legalism and hypocrisy, completely missing His grace. They were unable to see the revealed Son of God when He came because He was so different from what they expected.

The lives of the Pharisees were a testimony of human effort rather than of God's saving grace and mercy. What they achieved, they achieved on their own.

▶   *The important thing to them was what they were doing for God, not what God had done for them.*

The Pharisees rejoiced in their own works. Their lives had man's imprint upon them not God's, and subsequently lacked His life and power. It was just religion! Their lives strayed from God's plan and purpose in the same way that the life created by Abraham and Hagar missed it. Their lives also fell short of God's divine order in the same way that the oxcart built by David failed to achieve His best. The Pharisees hindered God from moving in their midst by trying to do it all themselves. They might have been good men, but one cannot say they were godly men. So caught up were they in their human reasoning and effort that, when God came in person, they didn't recognize Him and even believed Him to be their enemy. They went to their graves with Jesus' blood on their hands, never realizing what they had done and what they had missed.

▶   *They chose what seemed good, and in so doing, missed what was God!*

Looking ahead

About a year ago, the Lord gave me a vision. I could see a raging fire. It was burning across the top of a ridge, burning the high places, engulfing an entire village of wood shanty houses that had been erected there. I sensed it was a fire from God. When I asked Him the meaning of it, He showed me that the little shanties represented our pitiful human effort to do for ourselves what we are not willing to wait for God to do. The row upon row of wooden shanties represented the accumulation of months and years of our self-effort, human logic and wisdom, self-protection, self-seeking, human thinking and so on. They represented *the way that seems right to a man* that we have all embraced in many areas of our lives. God's desire is to burn it all up by the power of His Spirit so that the ground of our hearts is laid bare for Him to build upon. It is only wood, hay and stubble anyway! These shanties I saw are built upon the high places of our hearts as we have worshiped false gods by putting our trust in things other than the Lord. He wants to tear down and burn these altars to Baal that we have set up in our hearts through the years. He wants the Ishmaels, the oxcarts, and the pharisaical approach to go, to be thrown as firewood upon His altar.

It is a new day! The stone is rolled away and Jesus Christ is being revealed in this earth as the King of kings and the Lord of lords. As we seek Him in everything – what to say, what to do, how to respond, when to move, for every step, every moment of every day – He will establish Himself as our King and Lord. As we differentiate between what is merely good and what is actually God's thinking and leading, His kingdom will increasingly be established and be released in our lives and in this earth. His inheritance will be realized in our lives in a greater way!

Prayer

Dear Lord, in many areas of my life I have been following the way "that seems right" rather than Jesus, who is *the Way* (John 14:6). I have been depending largely upon my own human reasoning and logic, rather than seeking Your mind, heart and will in every matter. I have also been depending upon my own human effort and strength rather than the power and enabling that comes from Your Spirit within me. Please forgive me, Lord, for falling short of the mark and missing Your best for my life as I have operated independently of You. I receive Your forgiveness for the Ishamaels I have created as I have impatiently gone ahead with my own plan instead of waiting for Yours. I receive Your forgiveness for the new oxcarts I have built when I did not seek Your strategy and method. I receive Your forgiveness for living like a

Pharisee, choosing what *seemed* good and right, but completely missing You in the process. Lord, I invite You to cleanse me with Your Holy Fire today. Cleanse me of all that wood, hay and stubble in my life. Cleanse me of all unrighteousness, I pray. Burn it up! I give You all of my self-effort and human reasoning, placing those things upon Your altar. Consume my sacrifice, Lord, as I commit today to follow You with a whole heart and to seek You in everything. I choose to place my hand in Yours today and allow You to lead and guide my every step. I choose to be yoked with You. Where You lead, I will follow. Amen.

Chapter 15

Penetrating, Exploding, Transforming Passion

"My soul longs, yes, even faints
For the courts of the LORD;
My heart and my flesh cry out for the living God."

(Psalm 84:2)

The Lord gave me a vision one night many years ago that changed my life. I was at a fancy ball, standing on the sidelines watching the couples dancing. They were all beautiful people, dressed in finery, elegantly swaying around the room as a full orchestra played upon a raised dais to one side. I was dressed for the ball in a lovely gown, but I felt frumpy compared to the others. It seemed only fitting that they were the ones on the dance floor and I was the one watching from the sidelines.

Suddenly, however, the dancing stopped and the crowd parted like the Red Sea in front of me, all the way along the dance floor. It left a corridor down the middle, with the crowd on each side, all looking expectantly to the other end. At the end of this corridor was a man. He was simply standing there, gazing at me from across the room. In fact, He had eyes for no one in the room but me! He began to walk towards me through the corridor of people, never taking his eyes off of me. I could not take my eyes off of him either! He was the most beautiful thing I had ever seen. Though he looked nothing like any artist's conception of Him, I knew it was Jesus. Eventually He reached me. He took me gently in His arms and looked down into my face with the most amazing love I had ever experienced. The longing that was in His eyes for me was almost beyond comprehension. I kept thinking,

"He could have chosen anyone else in this room but He chose me!" It was puzzling, yet breathlessly exhilarating.

The next thing I knew, we were the ones dancing, now alone on the floor as everyone else watched. But I was not really aware of the others. The entire room was a blur. In fact, my whole life became a blur as my awareness focused in only one direction – the Person who held me in His arms. Years later, I would learn a worship song with these words,

> " . . . When my will becomes enthroned in Your love,
> When all things that surround become shadows in the
>   light of You, I worship You."

When I first heard the song, I immediately remembered this vision because the words of the song describe exactly what was happening! Everything around me paled in significance in the light of my Lord. I was aware only of the probing intensity of His passion directed toward me, the unquenchable response of my heart and my soul to Him, and the security I felt as He held me tightly in His arms. Nothing else and no one else existed outside of the cocoon woven by His love around me.

When I awakened, coming back to reality with a start, I realized I would never be the same. My relationship with the Lord was changed forever! He was now not only my Savior and my God, but He was also my Love. The touch of His gaze upon my life changed me in ways I was not even aware of until much later. Looking back, I could see that some things were resolved in my life that night. God's love for me and commitment to me were settled. I knew I was accepted by the Beloved, regardless of how unworthy I felt. It gave me a new confidence to press into His presence. I wanted to be with Him in a way I never had before. His passion transformed me from a shy, reserved Christian, always holding back, to a blooming bride, full of desire for Him! Divine love was awakened within me.

Called to a love relationship

Many of us know Jesus as our Savior, Master and Lord, yet our walk with Him will not be complete until we also know Him as our Bridegroom.

► *We will not discover the fullness of the inheritance He has for us until
we come to know Him as our Love.*

Just as a diamond has many facets, and each one contributes to
the beauty of the whole, so there are many facets to the Lord's
relationship with us. This love relationship is *key*, yet it is a facet
of our walk with Him that is never experienced by many
Christians! They are content to be housemates, business partners,
or friends with the Lord, when He wants to also be their lover and
the object of their passion. Sadly, too many of us save our passion
for football games, or our interests such as music, art or travel.
What are you passionate about? Is He at the top of the list?

The Song of Solomon is the most striking example of this love
relationship with God seen in the Old Testament. There are a
number of different perspectives on this book, also called Song
of Songs and Canticle of Canticles. The allegorical one is favored
by the Jews and by many leading scholars in modern times. In
the allegorical interpretation, it is considered a poem descriptive
of the love between Jehovah and Israel (Jewish version), or
between Christ and the believer (Christian version). The key
word throughout the book is "beloved". The key verse might be
considered Song of Solomon 6:3:

> *"I am my beloved's
> And my beloved is mine."*

In the Old Testament, the Lord often spoke of Himself as the
husband of His people. Israel was portrayed as married to the
Father, but unfaithful and adulterous, serving other gods who
began to take His place in their hearts. If we are careless, the same
thing can happen to us! When we look for our comfort, our
security or our provision in something other than the Lord, it is a
form of idolatry. That means something as innocent as food can
become an idol to us if food is what we run to for comfort instead
of running to Him! Further, anything that controls us is also an
idol because we are bowing down to it in servitude. Fear is a good
example of another god we can serve without meaning to do so,
allowing it to rule and reign over us. From the Lord's perspective,
this too, is adultery.

A dear friend of ours once shared with us a story related to her by another friend. Her friend, a woman, had a very honest time with the Lord one day, pouring out her complaints to Him about the husband He had given her. Apparently, she went on at great length about her frustration and disappointment with this man. When she finally stopped, the Lord was silent for a moment. Then He spoke very quietly to her, saying, "I know. I have been living with an unfaithful spouse too."

In the gospels of the New Testament, John the Baptist referred to Jesus as a bridegroom (John 3:28–29). Jesus referred to Himself this way as well (Luke 5:33–35). Correspondingly, in various New Testament epistles, the Church is portrayed as betrothed *and* married to the Son. In western society, betrothal and marriage are two different steps and mean different things. However, the lines between the two were blurred in ancient Hebrew culture. The betrothed parties were, in many ways, legally in the position of a married couple. Unfaithfulness in the time between betrothal and consummation of the marriage was considered adultery just as if they had been married for years (Deuteronomy 22:23; Matthew 1:19). The marriage ceremony and supper were simply concluding festivities! In the Lord's eyes, we are *legally* married to Him as His bride because He purposed and ordained this union from before the foundation of the world. From His perspective, it is finished! This understanding is supported by the verses in the New Testament in which Jesus is called a bridegroom. The Greek word used is one that refers equally to one betrothed or to a newly married man.

A glimpse of marriage from the divine perspective

Human marriage is meant to be a picture of our relationship with God. When we use the term "marriage" it conjures a picture in each of our minds. If our experience with marriage or dating has been painful, the last thing we want is intimacy with a God who says He wants to be our husband! We will give lip service to the relationship with Him, but we will never allow ourselves to be vulnerable. Trusting God will be a major issue. We will find it difficult to really love Him with a whole heart. The saying, "Risk not, love not," highlights the truth that loving anyone engenders some degree of risk. We cannot love without opening our hearts and becoming vulnerable to hurt. Subsequently, those who have experienced hurt in human relationships will find it difficult to be vulnerable and experience the depth of what God has for them in a relationship with Him. Even *good* marriages, however, still fall far short of what the Lord has purposed us to share with Him! Every earthly marriage is imperfect because both parties are flawed. We cannot come close to fathoming what our perfect God desires in our relationship with Him unless we seek Him and allow His Holy Spirit to open our eyes and hearts. As the Apostle Paul shared with the Corinthian church,

> *"But as it is written:*
>
> > *'Eye has not seen, nor ear heard,*
> > *Nor have entered into the heart of man*
> > *The things which God has prepared for those who love Him.'*
>
> *But God has revealed them to us through His Spirit. For the Spirit searches all things, yes, the deep things of God."*
>
> (1 Corinthians 2:9–10)

It is necessary that we each delve into His Word for ourselves and discover what God has purposed for us as His bride. It is part of our godly inheritance! In Hebrew marriages, the marriage contract was called the *ketubah*. It was a written document stating the bride price, the rights of the bride and the promises of the groom. The Bible, as a legal document, is in many respects a contract of marriage that describes the covenant made between God and us. Testament is simply another word for covenant. In our Bibles, we have an old covenant and a new covenant! The marriage contract set out the bride price. This bride price was called the *mohar*. It was paid by the father of the groom and reflected the value of the bride. The New Testament, which we might describe as the new and improved marriage contract for the people of God, describes plainly the bride price paid for us. Our *mohar* was the life of the Son! The Father paid with His Son's life to gain us as His bride. That is how valuable each one of us is to Him!

Called to intimacy

As the bride we are called to a relationship of intimacy with the Lord. He intended for our relationship to be one of passion, longing, seeking and joyful sharing on the part of both bride and bridegroom. In the Song of Solomon, the Beloved says to the Shulamite,

> *"You have ravished my heart,*
> *My sister, my spouse;*
> *You have ravished my heart*
> *With one look of your eyes."*   (Song of Solomon 4:9)

We ravish *His* heart! He melts when He looks upon us. We are each the apple of His eye. He passionately adores us and longs for the time we are alone with Him. He knocks on the door of our hearts, saying, *"Open for me, my sister, my love"* (Song of Solomon 5:2). He stands behind the walls we have erected around ourselves, gazing through the lattice longingly at us. He speaks to each of us and says, *"Rise up, my love, my fair one, and come away!"* (Song of Solomon 2:13). He wants to kiss us and awaken the love within. He wants us to be as passionate about Him as He is about us!

Have you ever been in a one-sided relationship, knowing that you cared more for the other person than they cared for you? Or have you ever felt as though you were the one doing all the giving in a relationship? We will all agree that this kind of relationship is far from ideal. In fact, it can be frustrating, disappointing and painful. The Lord does not want to be in this kind of relationship with us. He does not want to be the One who loves more, cares more and gives more. He wants the love He has poured out upon us to be reciprocated! He wants us to adore Him and shower love back upon Him in wholehearted, passionate worship.

Called to bring forth life

As the bride of Christ, we are also called to a relationship of union with Him. Our Creator ordained that husband and wife were to become one flesh and cleave together (Genesis 2:24). The Hebrew means "cling to, stick to, become joined in union together". He was not only speaking of the joining together of human couples, but also of our spousal relationship with Him! The Apostle Paul spoke of this in 1 Corinthians 6:17 when he said, *"But he who unites himself with the Lord is one with him in spirit"* (NIV). The Lord wants us to be one with Him in a very real sense. He desires that we see as He sees, think the way He thinks, do as He would do, and operate according to His divine order in all things. His purpose is that we become conformed to the image of His Son (Romans 8:29), as He works in us to align us with His will and purposes (Philippians 2:13).

Jesus was the embodiment and fleshly expression of the Father to the world. He told people, "If you have seen me, you have seen the Father." The Lord's plan is that when people see us, they see Him as well! We are called the Body of Christ because He has purposed for Christ to be revealed to the world through us. Christ was first revealed to the world through a young virgin named Mary. The angel explained to her, *"The Holy Spirit will come upon you, and the power of the Highest will overshadow you"* (Luke 1:35). The Father planned to conceive His life in Mary and reveal Jesus, the *living* Word, through her by the power of His Spirit. He wants to do the same in us, though in a little different way! We see the first evidence of God's creative power at work as He gave birth to life in the book of Genesis. When the earth was formless and void, the Holy Spirit brooded over it until life came forth. The language used in this verse always brings to my mind a hen sitting on her eggs, incubating them until they hatch! Like the ancient earth, there are areas in our lives that are devoid of His life. They are devoid of *Him*. They are empty, barren, and fruitless.

▶ *The Holy Spirit wants to overshadow us and brood over us until His abundant life is manifested in our lives.*

There is a divine deposit He wants to make in each of us as we commune with and become one with Him. The Father wants to conceive the life of His Son in us by the power of His Holy Spirit, so that it is *"no longer I who live, but Christ lives in me"* (Galatians 2:20). He intends for Jesus to walk the earth again, in a sense, through each of us! The Holy Spirit was given permission by Mary to do His work in her. She responded to the news of God's plan and purpose by submitting her life to Him, saying, *"Let it be to me according to your word"* (Luke 1:38). What is our response to Him? Are our hearts likewise submitted?

Worship – an expression of the love relationship

There are many aspects to worship, some of which we see in the Hebrew and Greek words used in the original Bible texts. There are facets of service, of liturgy, sacrifice and celebration in worship. It also involves showing reverence, honoring the Lord and giving Him the glory that is due to Him. Yet another facet of worship involves our submission to Him. Jesus said, *"If you love Me, keep My commandments"* (John 14:15). He explained that our level of obedience and submission to Him will reflect the depth of love we have for Him. The heart submitted to God engenders an *attitude* of worship that transcends and eclipses the Sunday activity we call worship. The life surrendered to Him on His altar constitutes a *lifestyle* of worship that continually demonstrates to the Lord our love for Him.

Yet I believe that worship is meant to be so much more than submission and surrender! I have found in my own experience that worship based on obedience or obligation is boring and religious. Jesus did not come to bring us a religion but a relationship. Therein is the key to seeing His life and power permeate our lives and our worship!

▶ *When that love relationship with Jesus is at the center of it, worship becomes explosive, impacting, penetrating, transforming and uncontainable!*

As we come to understand the width and length and depth and height of the love of Christ that saturates our lives with the fullness of God (Ephesians 3:18–19), our worship deepens, broadens, expands and becomes more expressive.

▶ *When the love relationship with Jesus is at the center of our worship, there is a continual flow back and forth as we give to God and He gives to us.*

A heart full of passion needs to express that passion somehow. This is the real essence of worship. We minister to Him as He ministers to us, showering back upon Him the love that He has shed abroad in our hearts through the Holy Spirit.

Dr. Fuchsia Pickett, the well-known Bible teacher, has shared an experience she had as a young denominational minister. She was asked to minister in a church that was part of a different denomination. There, she was introduced to a dimension of worship she had never before encountered. She describes herself as sitting on the platform in "studied dignity", observing with fascination what was going on around her. Though the service seemed disorderly and almost irreverent by the standards with which she was familiar, it was obvious to her that these people deeply loved the Lord and were simply expressing that love, albeit in ways that seemed strange to her. One young woman caught her eye. She relates that, "Her face glowed as if it reflected a thousand-watt light bulb. Tears were flowing down her cheeks, and I heard her say, 'I love you, Jesus.'" Dr. Pickett goes on to share that the woman continued to whisper things to the Lord and that her face seemed to grow brighter and brighter. She climbed down off the platform and approached the woman three different times to whisper in her ear, hoping the young woman could explain to her what was happening. The woman, however, had her eyes closed and was so involved in what was transpiring between herself and the Lord that she was never aware of Dr. Pickett's presence. When she returned to the platform after her third try, the Lord spoke to her sweetly and told her, "Fuchsia, you can have that if you want it." Later, they continued the conversation in her room after the service. She asked the Lord, "Is that worship? Then what have I been doing all these years?" She says with some humor that the Lord was kind to her in His response, replying gently, "... you have simply been having religious services." At that, a cry rose up in her heart and tumbled from Her lips as she implored the Lord to teach her to worship.[1]

Worship – a vehicle for transformation

We find as we study the Scriptures that another facet of worship entails bringing the Lord an offering. We see a number of spiritual offerings mentioned in the New Testament. One is the sacrifice of praise. We bring Him our praise, the fruit of our lips, offering it to Him with reverent thanksgiving and celebration. The Lord has had me bring Him other kinds of offerings in my worship, however. These were things that did not seem so nice! In fact, they were quite ugly! At various and sundry times, He has asked me to bring Him my fears, the anger I was holding, rejection I had experienced, feelings of helplessness and confusion, my will, my inadequacy, the failure which was tormenting me, and so forth.

He told me that if I would give these things to Him, He would do a divine exchange and replace them with Himself. For my junk, He would give me His treasure! Out of the ashes of my life, He would bring beauty.

▶ *This divine exchange happens most often in the midst of worship.*

I don't mean specifically during a service in a church. I mean during a time when we are closeted away with the Lord in our hearts, giving to Him and receiving what He has for us. This can happen anywhere! In fact, I believe it the Lord's desire that we rest in this place continually, that it be our lifestyle. The Apostle Paul writes,

> *"But we all, with unveiled face, beholding as in a mirror the glory of the Lord, are being transformed into the same image from glory to glory, just as by the Spirit of the Lord."* (2 Corinthians 3:18)

Along with a lifestyle of worship, especially in those times of intense and passionate sharing, comes the ability to "see" with fresh eyes who God is and what He desires for us. In worship comes new understanding and revelation as the Holy Spirit unveils the things of God's kingdom. At the resurrection, the veil of the temple was torn in two, signifying that the presence of God behind the curtain would now be accessible to anyone at any time. This curtain also represented the body of Jesus that would be broken for us, that we might be restored to intimacy with the Father. As Hebrews 10 explains,

> *"Therefore, brethren, having boldness to enter the Holiest by the blood of Jesus, by a new and living way which He consecrated for us, through the veil, that is, His flesh ... let us draw near with a true heart in full assurance of faith ... "* (Hebrews 10:19–22)

We can come into the Lord's presence 24–7 to look upon His face and behold His glory. We can gaze upon Him whom we love, seeing Him as He is rather than what we may have created Him to be through our flawed human thinking. As we behold Him, the Scripture explains, we are changed into the same image. It is a well-known fact that we become more and more like the people with whom we spend our time. We are subtly influenced without our realizing it. This principle applies to time spent with the Lord as well.

▶ *The more time we spend with Him, beholding Him, the more like Him we become! We are transformed!*

Finally, through the transformation of His people, He brings a manifestation of His presence and His glory into the world. He is "lifted up" and exalted through our very lives, the result being that men are drawn to Him (John 12:32).

Stumbling blocks to intimacy and passionate worship

Dave and I have been married for twenty-three years. For a while when our children were young, we were so busy with parenting, work and Bible College that we became virtual strangers to one another. We felt like singles living in the same house or the proverbial "two ships that pass in the night". We still loved each other and even managed to catch a few hours together each week, but there was no romance in it. There was no intimacy. We were just two people living and working together. The passion was barricaded behind a towering wall of other commitments, pressures, deadlines, distractions and physical weariness. It took a weekend away to focus on our marriage exclusively, and a commitment to communicate again on a deep level, before we were able to recapture the intimacy and the passion that were part of our relationship as lovers.

We can find the same kind of isolation and lack of intimacy occurring in our relationship with the Lord. The same things that kill passion in a marriage are the very things that hinder passion in our relationship with Him! Busyness, misplaced priorities and exhaustion are certainly major culprits, but there are other things that play just as big a part. Dishonesty is one thing. Unfaithfulness is another. In our relationship with the Lord, unconfessed sin will be block the flow of intimacy. The psalmist declared,

> *"If I regard iniquity in my heart,*
> *The Lord will not hear."* (Psalm 66:18)

Isaiah spoke prophetically to the people of Zion,

> *"Behold, the LORD's hand is not shortened,*
> *That it cannot save;*
> *Nor His ear heavy,*
> *That it cannot hear.*
> *But your iniquities have separated you from your God;*
> *And your sins have hidden His face from you,*
> *So that He will not hear."* (Isaiah 59:1–2)

Unconfessed sin is always accompanied by guilt, unless our hearts are extremely hardened. They are inseparable, like two sides of the same coin! In my own life, I have found that guilt almost always leads me to put up walls that shut God out. Unresolved shame and the sense of unworthiness, as we saw in a previous chapter, will also prompt us to put up walls to hide ourselves from the Lord and run from intimacy with Him. Shame and guilt will keep us from being honest and transparent with Him. Worship without honesty and transparency is simply religiosity – going through the motions, mouthing the words, but keeping our hearts far from Him.

Apathy is another big passion-killer! The young people we worked with in the northeast of England had an expression they used to describe this attitude of the heart. They would say, "A canna' be bothered." This expression became somewhat of a joke among us, but in truth, it is no laughing matter. Apathy happens when self rules. It is the natural product of a life ruled by the flesh. Any relationship takes work and a commitment to give to the other person. Apathy, however, keeps us in a mode of selfishness so that we are unwilling to give of ourselves to the Lord to keep the relationship with Him vibrant and growing.

Entering into our destiny

Despite the subtle machinations of the flesh to deviate us from our divine destiny, we were *created* to worship! Before the fall of man and before sin ever entered the world to mar our relationship with our Creator, we existed in God's mind and heart as those He would create to declare His mighty works, show His glory and live in eternal fellowship and intimacy with Him. He is the very reason for our existence! A.W. Tozer recounted many years ago, during a series of messages on worship, a story about Brother Lawrence. As the dear old saint lay on His deathbed, he spoke to those gathered around him. "I am not dying," he told them. "I am just doing what I have done for the past forty years, and doing what I expect to be doing for all eternity!" Those around him asked, "What is that?" to which he replied, "I am worshiping the God I love!"[2]

Tozer's own definition of worship developed from a lifetime of walking with God. Before he died, he felt compelled to share with others what he had learned about worship and the relationship we are called to have with our Lord. Tozer wrote,

▶ *"True worship is to be so personally and hopelessly in love with God, that the idea of a transfer of affection never even remotely exists."*[3]

Have you discovered this kind worship for yourself? Have *you* found your destiny? I pray that you will continue to seek Him until the kiss of His lips awakens love within you, that the hidden riches of His kingdom found in true worship might become yours!

Prayer

Precious Father, I am crying out for You to open the eyes of my heart! I want to seek You with a whole heart. I desire to *know* the width, length, depth and height of Your love for me, and to *know* the love of Christ, that my life might be permeated with the fullness of God (Ephesians 3:18–19). Lord, I confess any apathy to You which has locked me in a mode of selfishness, unwilling to put the effort into our relationship. I confess everything to You that has missed Your mark of holiness or excellence in my life. [Be specific about anything not brought to Him previously.] I place those areas of sin under the Blood of Jesus, receiving Your forgiveness and cleansing. Thank You, Lord, for bringing new understanding and revelation of who You are and how much You love me, as I worship You. I pray that You will heal anything in my life that has opened a door for a fear of intimacy. I open my heart to You now and invite You to do that work of healing. I renounce fear as an enemy! I desire a relationship of intimacy and union with You and choose to stand against anything that would hinder such a relationship from developing to its full potential. I dedicate my spiritual ears to You, Lord, and ask that You would free them from any deafness caused by Satan in my life. I want to hear Your sweet words of life whispered to my soul. I also want to feel Your kiss upon my lips and the beat of Your heart next to mine. Awaken Your love within me, dear Lord. Awaken the passion that lays dormant within me! I want to know you as my Bridegroom and as the Love of my life! Amen.

Notes

1. Fuchsia Pickett, *Worship Him* (Creation House, Lake Mary, FL, 2000), pp. 1–3.
2. A.W. Tozer, *Whatever Happened to Worship?* (Kingsway Publication, Eastbourne, England, 1985), p. 45.
3. Ibid., p. 29.

Chapter 16

Being a Blessing Brings Blessing

Walking in our godly inheritance means walking in blessing. The blessing of the Father is part of His Kingdom. Yet, few of us experience the depth of blessing in our lives that I believe our heavenly Father desires to shower upon us. Why is this? While there may be a number of reasons for this situation, a primary reason concerns our inability to understand the way the spiritual universe works. There are spiritual laws and principles at work in our lives in the same way that natural laws and principles govern things in the physical world.

▶ *Many Christians are unaware of God's spiritual pattern and order. Consequently, we often unwittingly violate His spiritual principles and do not place ourselves in a position where His blessing can be manifested in our lives.*

One of my mentors used to say, "Get under the spout where the glory comes out!" What I understood her to mean was, "Find that dimension where His grace and blessing is released and stand in that place." It is a matter of adjusting to God, and to His laws and principles, rather than expecting Him to adjust to us. Much of the time we expect to go about our business, doing what we want to do the way we would do it, expecting God to bless us. He certainly desires to bless us, and is releasing blessing in the heavenly realm (Ephesians 1:3), but all too often we have not put ourselves in the position to receive it!

The Lord illustrated this to me just the other day. I was cutting up some moving boxes and there were little pieces of Styrofoam floating around that had been inside the boxes. They kept sticking to me! I was picking them off and trying to get rid of them but they were so supercharged with static electricity that they would instantly stick to me again. In fact, they would literally jump on me over the space of several inches! The Lord nudged me and said, "My blessing is like this." I quit playing with the Styrofoam and started listening. He went on, "When you put yourself in the position to receive My blessing, you are charged up with the power of My Spirit, and when My blessing is poured out it gravitates and sticks to you just like the Styrofoam!"

Giving places us under the spout of blessing

One place where God's glory and blessing are released to shower upon us is in giving. When we give, we place ourselves in a position to receive His blessing. I spoke in the last chapter about giving our love to the Lord in passionate worship, and how that releases His life and blessing in our lives as a result. However, there are other areas besides worship where our giving releases His blessing!

For example, God promises that if we will give faithfully to Him of our tithes and offerings, He will pour out blessing in our lives. He challenged the Israelites to quit robbing Him and bring their tithes into the storehouse. Then He promised them,

> *" ' . . . And try me now in this,'*
> *Says the LORD of hosts,*
> *'If I will not open for you the windows of heaven*
> ***And pour out for you such blessing***
> ***That there will not be room enough to receive it.***
> *And I will rebuke the devourer for your sakes,*
> *So that he will not destroy the fruit of your ground,*
> *Nor shall the vine fail to bear fruit for you in the field . . .*
> ***And all nations will call you blessed,***
> *For you will be a delightful land,'*
> *Says the LORD of hosts."*   (Malachi 3:10–12)

Finances, however, are only one area where giving brings blessing! Generous giving in *every* area of our lives will open the door for blessing and for more of our godly inheritance to be realized. In other words, "Being a blessing brings blessing!" Jesus said this about giving and blessing,

*"Give and it will be given to you: good measure, pressed down, shaken together, and running over will be put into your bosom. **For with the same measure that you use, it will be measured back to you.**"*   (Luke 6:38)

Ministers frequently use this passage to teach on monetary giving, but this was not the context of Jesus' remarks. He was actually talking about our dealings with other people! The Apostle Paul similarly wrote to the Corinthians,

*"But this I say: He who sows sparingly will also reap sparingly, **and he who sows bountifully will also reap bountifully.**"*
(2 Corinthians 9:6)

Paul understood the spiritual principle of sowing and reaping, explaining that generous giving and blessing will open a door for abundant blessing in our own lives.

A friend of mine in Florida also understands the principle that being a blessing brings blessing. At one point in her life, everything was crumbling around her. Her marriage was on the rocks. Her husband had found someone else that was more like the person he wanted her to be. Her son had just gone public with some shocking admissions about his own life and affairs that caused her great distress. She had lost the support of her church family over these things and felt very alone. Yet, in the midst of this heartache and tribulation, we received countless emails from her encouraging us in the work we were doing, praying for us and asking how she could help. During this horrendous time of her life, she took time and spent money that I know she did not have to mail hundreds of dollars worth of vitamins to our family on the mission field. Though the difficulties are easing up only slightly for her at this time, I know she will weather these trials and will emerge in the grace and power of the Holy Spirit. Why I am so sure of this? It is because she has placed herself as a giver under the spout where His glory comes out!

A poverty mentality blocks the flow of blessing

So often, however, a poverty mentality permeates our lives which makes it difficult for us to become real givers. We are not only stingy with our money, but we are miserly with our emotions, our time, our energy and how much of ourselves we give to God! I have noticed that those who see themselves as victims are more prone to live out of a poverty mentality and miss the blessing that comes with a generosity of spirit and a lifestyle of giving. Dave and I have lived in places where whole regions were affected by this victim spirit. When that spirit is operating, people tend to be inward-focused, self-absorbed, self-ish, and self-centered, unless the Spirit of God has done a mighty work of grace in their hearts and lives! They sit at home all day feeling sorry for themselves, lamenting what little they have and how ill-treated they are, as they wallow in their misery. They are always seeking encouragement and prayer from other people but rarely encourage or pray for anyone else. Their lives are characterized by taking, rather than giving and it actually *blocks* God's hand from releasing His blessing in their lives.

However, the Apostle Paul wrote to the Corinithian church saying that it is not about what *we* have. It is about what *God* has. His resources are available to us in order to fill the lack in every area of our lives! All of us can become extravagant givers regardless of our natural circumstances, because He is Jehovah Jirah, the Lord who provides the seed with which to sow. Paul explained,

> *"Now he who supplies seed to the sower and bread for food will also supply and increase your store of seed and will enlarge the harvest of your righteousness. **You will be made rich in every way so that you can be generous on every occasion**, and through us your generosity will result in thanksgiving to God."*
> (2 Corinthians 9:10–11, NIV)

I used to be controlled by a victim spirit that established a poverty mentality in my life. I heard someone say many years ago, however, that we often give *out* with a mere bucket full and expect to be given *to* with a truckload. Their statement described me perfectly and the conviction I experienced at that time set me on a course of change, away from the poverty mentality and towards a lifestyle of giving. I still have a long way to go in learning to be an extravagant giver, but it is something I am committed to working on with the Lord.

In the footsteps of Jesus

One Bible verse God has used in my life to bring a greater awareness of His call to extravagant giving is John 10:10 where Jesus says He came to this earth to give us *"abundant life"*. The Greek word used in the original language of the New Testament means "life that is excessive, overflowing, superabundant, over and above, more than enough, profuse, extraordinary and more than sufficient".[1] If Jesus came to bless so outrageously, how can I settle for giving less? He lives in me and wants to continue to bring this kind of abundant blessing to others through me. It is part of His nature to give lavishly and He desires that nature to be a part of who I am. If Jesus is characterized by a generosity that defies boundaries, this kind of generosity should characterize my life as well!

The key is to get our eyes off ourselves and onto Jesus. As we behold Him, He will transform us into His image (2 Corinthians 3:18). Our awareness will be of His abundance rather than of our lack. We will also be more sensitive to His leading as He directs us to the people He wants us to reach out to in giving of ourselves. We will hear more clearly His direction regarding how and when to give and His strategy for being a blessing. As we focus our eyes on Him, He will help us in our endeavor to develop an attitude and a lifestyle of extravagant giving whether it is in our finances or with time, encouragement, a listening ear or a helping hand.

Wrong motives can also hinder the flow of blessing

A caution is necessary, however, when we couple a discussion of giving with the flow of God's blessing. It is easy to fall into the trap of seeing it as a formula and begin to give, in order to receive! James addressed this issue indirectly. He explained that we ask and do not receive because our motives are wrong (James 4:2). The same spiritual principle works in giving. We will give and not receive if our motives are selfish and we are looking for what we get out of it.

Sometimes we also give in order to feel better about ourselves. Again, our motive in giving or being a blessing in this regard is selfish. None of us are exempt from this snare because we are all human and our old carnal nature is still alive and well to some degree! But Jesus was moved by compassion, not the need to feel better about Himself. His motives were completely selfless and His heart was directed towards the people He ministered to, not what He needed.

Christians can also give and bless others out of sense of duty. Again, our motives are skewed. In this instance, we are adhering to the letter of the law but completely missing the spirit or the heart behind it! We are focused on doing good works, rather than on allowing Jesus to be manifest in us and through us (2 Corinthians 4:10–11). The Bible does say that we were created for good works. However, the Lord desires those good works to flow out of His nature and character within us. Too often, our good works are the result of our attempt to earn brownie points with Him, look spiritual, or live up to some standard devised by the religious system!

Again, the key is to keep our focus on Jesus, not on ourselves or the people around us.

▶ *If our gaze rests upon Him, His Spirit will continually adjust and fine-tune our motives.*

As we look to Him, He will keep us in the place where the outpouring of His blessing sticks to us and permeates our lives!

How I came to learn the truth about giving for myself

When I was in Bible College, I came to a point during my second year where I was weary of life, apathetic, depressed and experiencing a severe lack of motivation. I dragged myself through each day doing only what I had to do to make it through the day and honor my commitments. There was little joy in it and my enthusiasm for Bible College and life in general had waned significantly.

One day I was praying about my pathetic life, asking the Lord what was wrong and what I could do to change things. In response, He began to speak to me about the Sea of Galilee and the Dead Sea (also called the Salt Sea). He reminded me of the disciples who had made a living fishing on the Sea of Galilee and all the instances mentioned in the New Testament about the fish caught there. He showed me that the Sea of Galilee was teeming with fish because water flowed in and water flowed out. It had an outlet. Then He directed me to read about the Dead Sea. I found that water flowed into the Dead Sea and stopped there. There was no flow of resources in and out. It had no outlet. As a result, minerals and salt accumulated to such a level that it was lethal to plant and animal life. It was dead in a very real sense.

The Lord then told me, "You are like the Dead Sea right now. You are only concerned with your own life and what is being required of you. You are not giving out at all. There is a tremendous flow into your life right now but no flow out. This is why you feel so dead and lifeless!" At His leading, I became more sensitive to the outlets for giving that He was bringing across my path. As a result, blessing was released in my life.

▶   *The more I poured out, the more God poured in!*

My enthusiasm was renewed. I felt charged up, invigorated and suffused with fresh life. I began to see God's hand moving once again in my life and became more aware of His all-sufficient grace supporting me and enabling me to stand. I looked forward once again with faith and expectancy to what each day would bring. I learned firsthand during this season of my life that being a blessing brings blessing!

Prayer

Dear Father, I humbly desire to seek and serve You in a way that will bring blessing in the lives of others. I want to become a giver of my time, my resources, my compassion, and my very life! In fact, Lord, I want to follow in Your footsteps and allow extravagant giving to become a part of who I am. I want Your nature and character to infiltrate my life so that I am more like You in every way. I pray that the Father's blessing would be released in my life in a fresh way as I focus the eyes of my heart upon You alone. Let there come a fresh measure of that blessing and let it be worked into my life in a deeper way. Help me to learn to stand in that spiritual place where I am able to receive Your glory and blessing, and where every fiber of my being is permeated by Your life and power. I pray that as I pour out according to the leading of Your Holy Spirit, You will pour back in abundantly – good measure, pressed down, shaken together and running over! I invite You to fine-tune my every motive in giving, Lord, that I might not give out of obligation or guilt, to feel better about myself or in order to receive. I pray that You would purify my motives, that they would glorify You in every way. Thank You for being a God of abundant provision and blessing. It is a privilege and an honor to serve You! Amen.

Note

1. *Spirit Filled Life Bible,* Jack Hayford gen. ed. (Thomas Nelson Publishers, Nashville, 1991), p. 1593.

Chapter 17

Here Comes the Bride!

Many years ago, at the instigation of my pastor, I read a book that revolutionized my walk with the Lord. It was entitled *Destined for the Throne* and was written by a radio pastor and Bible College president named Paul E. Billheimer.[1] The book is described on its title page as,

> "A study in biblical cosmology setting forth the ultimate goal of the universe which is the Church reigning with Christ with a new view of prayer as 'on-the-job' training in preparation for the throne."

The author painted such a clear picture in this book of our eternal purpose that I had a vision for the first time of what the Christian life is all about. Up to that point, I had just been existing day to day, with little momentum or direction in my walk with God. I struggled with where I was going and with finding a frame of reference for what the Lord was doing in my life. I've heard it said that if you don't know where you are going you will never get there. That certainly describes my life at the time! I drifted from one church service to the next, but nothing seem to particularly impact or change me in a big way. I knew that I was not gaining any new ground. As I read *Destined for the Throne*, I was energized by the new revelation that the Lord was bringing in my spirit. It brought purpose and meaning to my existence and to my Christian walk! What the Lord showed me gave me a context for the new chapters He was writing in my life. The loose puzzle pieces began falling into place and things that confused me began to make sense. It became much easier to accept and walk through the difficulties I encountered because I could see that there was a purpose in them. Understanding the "bigger picture" helped me to move forward and grow in my walk with the Lord as I answered the call to be His bride and began to discover the practical realities of His eternal kingdom!

Preparation of a bride

God is preparing the Church as a bride for Himself. The King of kings intends to have a Queen at His side to share in His dominion and authority! He is preparing each of us personally for an eternity of ruling and reigning with Him (2 Timothy 2:12; Revelation 5:10; 22:4). Because we are called to share His throne and His glory, there is a preparation process in which all believers are involved. Jesus is coming for a bride without spot or wrinkle (Ephesians 5:27). That means the Holy Spirit is committed to working in us until we are the exact image of Jesus! I know that I am personally nowhere close to this image. I am still a roadway under construction. The Holy Spirit's heavy equipment is plowing through the middle of my life, gouging out a path and cutting deep furrows through the hillside of my heart. I know I am still a bit of a mess! However, we are all in this process together as the bride in whom He is working. Philippians 1:6 encourages us that He will complete the good work He has begun in us. He is so faithful not to leave us under construction, but is forever working to move us towards completion and perfection. He is continually challenging, compelling, and wooing us to a higher, deeper and broader place, anticipating that we have our spiritual ears open and are tuned in to His frequency!

The outworking of this preparation process in our lives moves us ever closer to stepping more fully into our godly inheritance.

▶ *Just as the Israelites pressed into the land of promise and possessed it step by step, **the more we yield to the Lord's preparation process in our lives, the more we will possess our spiritual inheritance!***

As we yield to His work, a greater measure of His glorious kingdom will infiltrate, penetrate and saturate our lives.

A number of years ago, I undertook to study in depth the book of Ephesians. I found that this New Testament epistle portrays the Church as a very unique kind of bride – a bride wearing combat boots! We have the unique distinction of being a bride who is called to warfare. A friend of ours named Steve Schultz wrote a book several years ago about the military-type training process the Lord is committed to working in each of our lives.[2] Steve mentions 2 Timothy 2:3,

> *"You therefore must endure hardship as a good soldier of Jesus Christ."*

What transforms a young man or woman off the street into a soldier is the hardship of the rigorous training he or she is put through. Think about the soldiers in the British SAS or the American Green Berets, Rangers or SEALS. Have you ever wondered about the kind of intense training they must endure to become such crack troops? The training is hard. It is painful. It is intense. However, when the training period finally reaches an end the troops are usually tough, committed and extremely effective as the military force they are called to be. Our lives on this earth are a training period for eternity. The Lord is working tenacity, strength, commitment and effectiveness into His troops. He is preparing us to be a radical warrior bride!

Running from the preparation is problematic!

Sometimes soldiers go AWOL. They cannot handle the rigors of the boot camp or training experience, so they run away. Many of us have gone AWOL from the boot camp in which we have found ourselves with the Lord. We have "checked out" and escaped by burying ourselves in work, in school, sports, music, relationships or any unlimited numbers of other things. We are still wearing our uniform but we have distanced ourselves from the drill field and the voice of our instructor. Those who run away never discover the benefits of pressing through the training, however. Hebrews 12 tells us,

> *"... God disciplines us for our good, that we may share in his holiness. No discipline seems pleasant at the time, but painful. Later on, however, it produces a harvest of righteousness and peace for those who have been trained by it."*
>
> (Hebrews 12:10–11, NIV)

If we will persevere and stick with His program, we will reap His peace and His righteousness in our lives. We will reap the blessings of the Father and the rich reward of His bountiful inheritance.

There was a time in my life when I wanted to run away. I was recently reading through my journals from 1988 and found one entry that read in capital letters, "Lord, get me out of here! I can't take it anymore!" At that time, Dave and I were in Bible College in the Dallas, Texas area. The five years we spent there were the best *and* the worst time of my life! Dave and I were thirty-ish, with two young children in private Christian schools, a mortgage and a car payment. We were both trying to go to school full-time, be involved in church and ministry, and still work to pay the bills! What an impossible task. Sometimes I thought I would die! Additionally, the Lord was carefully kneading into my inner being everything I was learning in the Bible college classroom through His *own* classroom or training ground of daily life. He used every possible situation to show me that there were still responses in me that were not of Him. He took advantage of every opportunity to expose the ugliness, darkness and garbage still in my heart. He put me in one situation after another that would bring my rough edges to light so that He could file them off. I often felt as though the Lord was dunking me under water to the point of drowning, then letting me up for a breath of air before He dunked me again to continue to work His discipline into my life. It was intense, painful, and agonizing. Further, it went on for five long years! The end result, however, was worth it. I discovered that the peace and the righteousness of God had been worked into my life in greater measure because I stuck it out through that particular training period.

There was a later period in my life where I wanted to run away again. This time I was a pastor! The Lord had sent us to plant and pioneer a church in an area of the southwestern United States that was ruled by the occult and infested with a number of satanic and witchcraft covens. There was so much demonic activity going on that when ministry friends came to visit, they would make comments like, "The oppression is so heavy here, how are you able to keep breathing?" The first few years there were extremely difficult in many different ways. I was frequently ill. We experienced a great deal of turmoil and seemed to be up against a brick wall with the church. And as if that were not enough, we were targeted by some of the occult groups in the area for special attention! Dave and I were both keeping our spiritual ears open, hoping for a release from the Lord to move on to an easier place. It was that rough! However, the release never came during that difficult period and so we simply persevered. The Lord repeatedly encouraged me with Hebrews 10:36 (NIV), which says,

> *"You need to persevere so that when you have done the will of God, you will receive what he has promised."*

We began to concentrate our energy on prayerfully seeking the Lord for answers and for His direction instead of toying with the desire to run away. By the time the release came a number of years later, we no longer wanted to leave! We had learned the value of pressing through to breakthrough.

The process of training for reigning continues

Dave and I are still in training and so are you! None of us will ever be finished with the Lord's training and equipping process in this life. He will continue His work of preparation in each of us, training us for reigning over our own flesh, over the difficult circumstances of life and over the kingdom of darkness. As long as we keep ourselves under His hand and don't run away or pull back by putting up walls, His training will have its perfect work in us! We will also discover more fully the inheritance He has for us.

Each day is a day of decision. Our destiny awaits us.

▶ *Will we press through the preparation process to possess our inheritance and allow His kingdom to come in our lives more completely?*

Will we allow the Lord to shape us to become the mighty force in this world we are called to be? Will we arise from the dust and loose ourselves from the bonds that constrain us in order to fulfill our divine destiny?

As all creation awaits the return of the Bridegroom, I can almost hear the heavenly orchestra striking up the tune, "Here Comes the Bride". The great cloud of heavenly witnesses (Hebrews 12:1), are standing to their feet, eagerly watching for the restoration of all things and the approach of the Church towards the consummation of her eternal destiny. With the end of time and the return of our Lord imminent, it is my fervent prayer that we will approach each new day with eyes to see, ears to hear and a submitted heart as our King continues to prepare us to rule and reign with Him. I pray that His kingdom will come and His will may be done in each of our lives more completely as we press toward the goal for the prize of the upward call of God in Christ Jesus (Philippians 3:14).

Prayer

Dear Lord, thank You for the glorious destiny that awaits me as Your bride called to rule and reign with You for eternity. Thank You for the training and equipping that You are doing in my life each day as You prepare me for this holy and awesome calling. I choose to submit in a fresh way to Your work and Your discipline in my life. I ask Your forgiveness for any way in which I have resisted Your training process, run from it or gone AWOL. Please fill me anew with the divine enabling that comes from Your Holy Spirit. I pray You will strengthen me, Lord, and harden my resolve to walk after You fully that I might persevere through every trial and tribulation, through every disappointment and devastation, and through every obstacle and stumbling block I might encounter. I desire Your peace and Your righteousness to be worked into my life until they are a part of who I am. I desire to reveal Jesus in a greater way and invite You to do what it takes to conform me to that image. Lord, reveal Your glory through this humble, broken vessel. May Your kingdom come and Your will be done in my life more completely. May the godly inheritance You purposed for me from before the foundation of the world become more and more of a reality in my life as I seek Your face and seek first Your kingdom and Your righteousness. Amen.

Notes

1. Paul E. Billheimer, *Destined for the Throne* (Christian Literature Crusade, Fort Washington, PA, 1975).
2. Steve Schultz, *Radical Warriors Require Radical Training* (Christian International, Santa Rosa Beach, FL).

If you have enjoyed this book and would like to help us to
send a copy of it and many other titles to needy pastors in the
Third World, please write for further information
or send your gift to:

**Sovereign World Trust
PO Box 777, Tonbridge
Kent TN11 0ZS
United Kingdom**

or to the **'Sovereign World'** distributor in your country.

Visit our website at **www.sovereign-world.org**
for a full range of Sovereign World books.